The Raised Bed Book

The Raised Bed Book

The definitive step-by-step guide to elevated growing

David Hurrion

Contents

 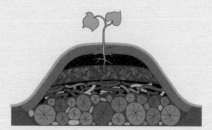 

Elevate your garden

Whether it's growing bumper crops of vegetables and fruit, creating a flower-filled plot, or adding stylish design elements to your garden, raised beds provide practical solutions to help you grow better.

Gardening has been a passion all my life, and anything that helps me to grow better plants has to be good news. And if they're thought through and designed for a purpose, raised beds can be just that. They provide proof that soil is the foundation for healthy plants, and so, whether you're a newbie gardener or a seasoned daughter- or son-of-the-soil, this style of growing is sure to make your gardening more productive and more rewarding.

The use of raised beds has many practical benefits, not only for the gardener, but also for the plants themselves, the design of our growing spaces, and, potentially, for our wildlife. As the Earth's resources and natural habitats come under ever-increasing pressure in the face of climate change, it is crucial that we learn how to use raised beds as effectively and sustainably as possible.

It is often said that "gardening is an inexact science". How plants respond to the soil, the prevailing weather, and what we do to them varies all around the world, and from plot to plot. In fact, no two gardeners will garden in the same way. With this in mind, I've aimed to write a go-to volume to help every grower find success with raised beds, in whatever kind of growing space they have.

So, whether you are deciding if you need to grow in raised beds in the first place and choosing what to grow in them, or if you're looking to understand the different methods of building and the essentials of a suitable growing medium, or even the basics of how to care for your plants and keep the soil in tip-top condition, you'll be sure to find inspiration in the following pages. Welcome to *The Raised Bed Book*. I hope you enjoy it!

About the author

David Hurrion has been a gardener all his life. Having trained and worked in horticulture he has an extensive knowledge and practical experience of plants, crops, and growing techniques in the UK and around the world. He regularly teaches, writes, and presents about gardening and growing, and has travelled extensively to see plants growing in their natural environments. David is also a Tender Ornamental Plant Committee member and Show Judge for the UK's prestigious Royal Horticultural Society, and currently gardens in the south of England. www.davidhurrion.com / Instagram: @davidhurrion YouTube: @davidhurrion

Raised beds aren't just for vegetables. They are a great way to enhance sloping sites, are easy to maintain, and can improve soil conditions to help you get the most from your growing space.

The fundamentals

A long-practised tradition

It's easy to think that gardening and growing in raised beds is a concept that has come about in the modern Western world, when homes and their outdoor spaces are getting smaller. So it may come as a surprise to learn that at least as far back as 550BCE, humans were cultivating plants in what amounts to large stone boxes, filled with the best soil.

Built at the behest of Nebuchadnezzar II, the Hanging Gardens of Babylon – listed as one of the Seven Wonders of the Ancient World – are some of the world's earlier raised beds, and existed to the south of Baghdad, in what is now Iraq. And they weren't just built for growing food: it seems these gardens also had ornamental value and were planted with trees to provide shade from the heat of the midday sun. In fact, they provided artificial oases to make life more elegant and pleasant, for a chosen few of course.

The biggest drive for creating raised beds, however, came from the practical necessity for crop growing, and this seems to have seeded itself independently, in disparate parts of the world, as different civilizations developed, along with the need to feed a large, concentrated population. The way these embanked growing structures were designed and used depended on the unique geography, climate, crops, and human needs of each civilization.

For some, like the Aztecs in Mexico and the people who pre-dated the Incas in South America, the rich soils of lake beds were cultivated in a series of broad, flat-topped mounds separated by open water channels. This allowed the top of the soil mounds to be free-draining and aerated – ideal for

Raised beds on a grand scale
– an artist's impression of the Hanging Gardens of Babylon.

plant roots to grow in – but retained a high water table in the underlying ground to keep the crops supplied with plentiful moisture to tap into. This system is most commonly associated with the Tiwanaku people around the shores of Lake Titicaca, in what is now Bolivia, where it is referred to as *waru waru* and dates as far back as 300BCE. Similar bed systems in Mexico were given the name of *chinampas*, dating back to at least 1200CE. In fact, similar systems are used today, referred to in Spanish as *camellones*.

Terraced beds

Meanwhile in the mountains of the Andes, most notably on the vertiginous drops of fifteenth-century Machu Picchu, complex land-sculpting was used by the Incas to create endless terraces in which to grow crops. Here, stone retaining walls were built into the rock face, then back-filled with layers of crushed stone and sandy soil, and topped with rich organic matter and manures to provide a productive growing medium.

The level terraced beds thus created were specifically designed to prevent soil washing away in this high-rainfall area, and to provide a means by which water can be encouraged to soak into the ground to reduce flooding. The flat surface enabled easy cultivation and optimized the use of land – both of which were essential in such mountainous conditions. In addition, the retaining walls, which could be as much as 5 metres (16½ft) in height, provided a "heat sink" whereby they would store the sun's warmth by day and radiate it back to the crops by night. This is the basis of our modern-day storage radiators.

Terracing is by no means unique to the mountains of South America. Variations on a theme have been used for hundreds, if not thousands, of years in South and East Asia, perhaps most notably in Neolithic southern China to create floodable paddy fields in which to grow rice. But they have also been and still are used to form level, more easily cultivated ground for a diverse range of vegetables and fruit.

Meanwhile in the southwestern United States, terracing was fundamental to retaining soil, to prevent it being washed away during times of

Terraced moutaintop at Machu Picchu, Peru, modelled for intensive growing in response to the challenges of the climate.

Historically, raised beds have been used to improve the growing conditions for specific crops.

Luxury of Gardens

Landscape designer Humphry Repton recognized the accessibility benefits of raised beds as early as 1816, as a wheelchair user himself.

seasonal high rainfall. One group of native people, the Anasazi, developed techniques of embankment across valleys and on hillsides using rocks and earth. Behind these structures rain-washed alluvium was encouraged to accumulate where it could be gradually enriched for cultivation, combined with dams to retain and control water flow at times of high rainfall. Descendants of these people, the Hopi, still use these techniques today.

European innovation

Variations of all these methods of embankment and terracing were developed throughout Europe, too, over thousands of years. Initially they took the form of simply growing crops on mounded beds of soil, which would allow excess moisture to drain away and enable the surface to be enriched with dressings of manure. These systems developed extensively in the successive Minoan, Greek, and Roman empires, and eventually started to make efficient use of more marginal lands for the cultivation of grapes and olives, using terracing on hillsides. These practices spread right around the shores of the Mediterranean.

In Medieval times – from around late 400CE through till 1450 or so – cultivation of arable crops centred around religious communities. In most cases it would involve growing in mounded beds of soil, and in some instances these would be held in place at the edges with short wattle panels.

By the late eighteenth century and the beginnings of the marked expansion of towns and cities, market gardens began to spring up around these centres of population to provide food for the workers. At a time when animals were the main means of transport, there was a ready source of manure, which allowed growers to develop productive mounded beds in which to grow all manner of vegetables and fruit.

Meanwhile in large country estates, teams of gardeners were employed to grow food for the "big house", including exotic crops that were being introduced to Europe from across the world. To this end, raised beds were often used to enrich the soil for intensive cropping or to create ideal growing conditions for particular crops, such as potatoes. The use of fresh, mounded manure to release heat as it decomposed was also employed in beds edged with timber or brick and covered with a glazed lid or "light". These "hot beds" (see page 130) could be used to grow very early-season vegetables or to provide additional warmth for the cultivation of exotic fruits, such as bananas and pineapples.

By the Regency period, the accessibility benefits were also being acknowledged by influential figures such as landscape designer Humphry Repton. And so the modern-day raised bed was born.

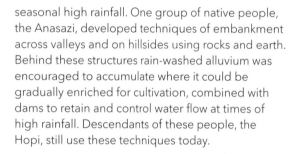

Raised beds and terracing have long been incorporated into the design of historic buildings, such as Christ Church, Oxford.

Why grow in raised beds?

Growing in raised beds offers all kinds of benefits – to the plants, to the soil, to the natural world, to the design of a plot, and to gardeners themselves.

Plants that need acidic soil, such as rhododendrons, can be well catered for in raised beds.

There are two key benefits of growing in raised beds that most people think of before any others. The first is accessibility – the option to tailor the height and width of beds to suit the needs of every differently abled, young, or elderly gardener.

The second is the connection between raised beds and vegetable growing. It has almost become de facto that new gardeners believe the only way to succeed with crops is to grow them in raised beds.

In both cases, of course, there are plenty of reasons why raised beds can be the better option, even though they are not essential, but there are plenty of other benefits besides these that raised beds bring to the table.

Growing in raised beds can be better for all sorts of different plants, can allow for creativity in garden design and layout, and can make life easier for the gardener, whatever their age or ability. As well as making better use of resources, growing in raised beds can also bring advantages to the natural environment. But in order for their benefits to be had, they do need to be carefully considered, planned, constructed, planted, and maintained.

Any method of organized growing relies on managing the growth of plants. This might be to get

the best crop or the most attractive flower display, or to create wildlife habitats. And ultimately this depends on the interaction between the plants themselves, the soil environment, the prevailing climate, and the gardener.

All of these factors need to be considered when choosing how, where, and what to grow, so much so that there is much written about "right plant, right place". And of course, battling against unfavourable conditions is likely to stress the plants and the grower: thin, sandy soil will not suit species that need lots of water and nutrients, causing them to grow weakly and be susceptible to pests and diseases; meanwhile, rich, moist conditions can cause some plants to grow in uncharacteristic ways and make them prone to rotting. Where the soil and conditions can't be changed, then, it pays to choose things that will be able to cope with them.

But there is also a lot to be said for "right plant, right soil", and raised beds filled with an appropriate growing medium to suit the plants allow the gardener more choice of what to grow.

Ultimately, choosing whether to grow in raised beds comes down to weighing up all the benefits, whether for the plants, the environment, the design of the growing space, or the gardener.

Growing vegetables in even low beds allows intensive cultivation through soil management and application of nutrients.

Benefits for plants

The best gardens and growing spaces are those where the plants and soil are suited to one another. Raised beds can provide the ideal environment, tailored to optimize conditions for the best results.

Plants are adapted to growing in specific native ground conditions, whether it be a moist, dense, rich root run in areas of high rainfall or dry, open, hungry soil in an arid region. Give each the opposite conditions and the moisture-loving plant will decline and fade, while the drought-adapted one will rot and die.

There are countless plants, each with their own set of soil and climate needs, but, of course, lots of species share broadly similar requirements. Gardeners and growers can take advantage of this to group these together to create planting schemes to suit the prevailing conditions in their plots. But when it comes to growing things that won't thrive, raised beds and tailored soils are the only option.

Take the example of border delphiniums. The statuesque, modern-day hybrids originate from combining genes from a wide range of different species, from diverse parts of the world – most notably the Swiss Alps, Siberia, Armenia, and the Himalayas. They are all deep rooting to allow them to survive cold winters and tap into moisture to support the tall stems and flowerheads. Breeding these species together, and selecting them over hundreds of years, has produced taller hybrids with immense, densely packed flower spikes, which are the envy of many gardeners.

In order to have any chance of success with these plant equivalents of thoroughbred racehorses, the soil will need to be deep, moisture-retentive yet aerated, with plenty of nutrients. Add in a seasonal cold spell to allow the plants to become dormant, and the reward of towering blooms could be within your grasp. It's no use trying to grow them on sandy, dry, impoverished soil in a subtropical climate: they just won't hack it.

Deep-rooting delphiniums benefit from a cool, moist root run in order to thrive.

Lifting plants with raised beds or terracing can bring them up into the light to optimize their growing conditions.

The majority of plants will benefit from at least half a day of full sunlight at the height of the growing season. Of course, this in turn means that they get shade for part of the day, hence the term "part shade", which is used to refer to the requirement of so many plants. "Dappled shade" generally means a position under the foliage of trees and large shrubs. But the biggest limitation to plant choice is a place in "full shade", where there is pretty much no direct light for the majority of the day.

Sites at the base of tall walls and fences facing due north in the northern hemisphere, or due south in the southern hemisphere, are most likely to get lots of full or deep shade,

although they may get direct light first thing in the morning and last thing in the evening. Using a raised bed to lift the growing level in such spots will benefit the plants by bringing them up higher, where they stand more of a chance of getting some diffuse or direct light. They can use this extra light to make more sugar via photosynthesis, which supports stronger and healthier growth.

Beds in full sun, filled with free-draining soil, can create ideal conditions for plants that like hot, dry conditions.

Group plants together that require similar soil and growing conditions to ensure that all will thrive. Avoid mixing plants that naturally grow in wildly different environments.

Here's where the logic of growing in tailored soil comes into play. And what better way to provide it than in a raised bed? It allows the creation of a deep root run, in a fertile, moisture-retentive growing medium, which is perfect for certain plants, particularly delphiniums.

By contrast, there are lots of other plant types that would need an entirely different root environment in order to simply survive, let alone thrive. Succulents, for example, hail from places where moisture is at a premium either all the time, or during certain seasons. Many of them are deep rooting so that they can tap into water way down in the ground, but those roots are mostly surrounded by free-draining, aerated soil.

This is especially the case for species that originate in deserts, where the growing medium consists of sand, grit, or gravel. These have a wide variety of other adaptations to help them conserve critical moisture. In fact, if the soil retains lots of moisture and nutrients, the plants will grow too soft, making them more prone to water loss, structural collapse, and pests and disease.

Soil depth

The extent to which roots penetrate the soil varies from plant to plant. Shallow, fibrous rooted species have adapted to grow in particular conditions. This includes not only shallow soils that have formed over particularly solid rock types, but also situations where only the upper part of the topsoil provides aerated conditions conducive to growth. Further down there may be insufficient air either due to the density of the soil or as a result of waterlogging.

Fibrous rooted species include many annuals and biennials as well as some types of herbaceous perennials, conifers, and certain shrubs. In most cases, these are unlikely to penetrate more than 40cm (16in) into the ground – many rooting more shallowly than this.

By contrast, most trees, as well as some shrubs and herbaceous perennials, are able to produce deep roots. In many instances these have evolved where deep soils exist in nature, or to take advantage of cracks and fissures in subsurface rocks in order to tap into water. Perhaps surprisingly, this is also the case with some alpine species, which, despite their small stature above ground, may have roots penetrating up to 1 metre (3¼ft).

As a rule of thumb small trees, medium to large shrubs, and fruit bushes need a minimum of 30–40cm (12–16in) of topsoil and at least 50–60cm (20–24in) of subsoil below that into which they can root for stability and moisture. Meanwhile, herbaceous perennials and small shrubs will benefit from at least a 30cm (12in) layer of topsoil over 30–40cm (12–16in) of subsoil. Vegetables, bedding plants, annuals, alpines, and wildflowers should all be happy with a minimum of 20cm (8in) of topsoil and 20cm (8in) of subsoil. The existing soil may be deeper than this. Where it is shallower, the case is made for installing a raised bed to add to the depth of topsoil. The minimum depths above are also worth bearing in mind where beds are to be built on solid surfaces.

Increasing the depth of soil
using terraces or shallow raised
beds provides stable, level
growing conditions for plants.

What is meant by poor soil?

Where ground conditions are lacking in some way, the grower will always have the get-out clause of "poor soil" to blame. In fact, however, all existing soils can be improved and maintained by the addition of organic matter, as we will see in more detail in Chapter 5.

The worst soils for growing plants are those that have been contaminated in some way by chemicals and an excess of waste material, but coming in a close second are those with no organic matter. This is the material that provides the building blocks for all forms of soil life.

Sandy soils are often referred to as poor, but these can either be improved by the addition of organic matter or used to grow plants that relish free drainage and aeration at the roots. At the other end of the spectrum, dense clay soils – although heavy and difficult to work – are far from poor; in fact, they are very rich in nutrients and have the ability to hold on to lots of moisture.

Building raised beds above any of these soils will effectively overcome their limitations, but the growing medium that is used to fill them needs to be of good quality and maintained by the addition of organic matter otherwise it, too, may become impoverished!

Standardized conditions

The natural variability of soil in a site can occur within just a few tens of centimetres; there can be patches with different levels of organic material, mineral matter, and nutrients. And over the space of a metre, growing conditions can change from heavy and wet to light and dry. The pH levels (see page 192) can also vary.

Where this is the case, exactly the same plant species can perform in quite different ways, in one place growing tall and floriferous, in another being stunted and producing little in the way of bloom.

Creating a level growing surface ensures that rainwater can soak into the soil evenly, without running off.

Protective measures

Growing in a restricted area makes it much easier to protect vulnerable plants and crops from extremes of weather or attack by pests and diseases.

You can protect against frost more conveniently in a raised bed by covering it with horticultural fleece, polythene, or cloches. You might also be able to make a purpose-built glazed lid, which can be lifted into place during cold weather.

In very hot conditions or bright sunshine, you could use a cover made of shade netting or closely spaced timber lathes attached to a frame to prevent scorching and reduce water loss.

When it comes to pests and diseases, the act of raising them up closer to eye level can make it easier to see when they are attacking the plant, and also to institute measures to control the pathogen. With a raised bed you can inspect the plants conveniently from above, but also readily from the sides, looking in through the foliage.

The big benefits, however, come in the way that plants can be protected from attack in the first place. First, a number of pests can be deterred by

the height of the structure, most notably slugs and snails, which are less likely to climb the sides of the raised bed and may simply crawl around the base of it. Second, the bed can be covered with netting or fine-gauge mesh, depending on the pest involved, to act as a physical barrier.

In addition, there is a benefit in being able to cordon off the entire bed with sheets of polythene if spraying is chosen as an option for pest and disease control. This means that the chemical can be contained in a limited area, and not drift to other parts of the garden or growing space.

Grouping pest-vulnerable crops together in a raised bed allows them to be easily covered with protective netting or mesh.

Such soil differences within the same bed can result in variable performance not only in flowers and foliage, but also in the quantity of harvest from fruit and vegetable crops.

Standardizing the growing conditions at the roots can be achieved by digging, moving, and mixing the soil over a wide area, but this may not be entirely successful where there is variation in underlying stone and mineral matter. Soil moisture levels can also vary widely in a relatively short distance – compare the top of a sloping site to the bottom, for example.

Making a raised bed and filling it with layers of standardized materials (see page 194) will result in more even growing conditions. It will help to mask the influence of underlying rocks, minerals, and nutrients, as well as reducing the variability in moisture. The key thing to remember, however,

is that raising soil-surface level in a bed will accentuate the ability of the soil to drain.

Creating a flat, level soil surface in a well-constructed raised bed will also catch water, allowing it to drain in and keep the ground evenly moist to benefit all plants equally. In addition, it prevents run-off elsewhere and helps to stop soil erosion on a sloping site.

Fill a raised bed with a standardized topsoil mix to ensure that rooting conditions are the same for all the plants. This gives them the best chance of performing equally.

Water table matters

The structure of soil is crucial for providing air as well as moisture around the roots of plants, which is naturally provided by a combination of mineral and organic matter.

Air spaces between soil particles

Fibrous roots with fine root hairs, which absorb water from soil

Fibrous organic matter particles with water in organic matter "sponge"

Mineral matter particles with water held around edges by surface tension

The height at which free water exists in the soil is referred to as the water table. This is the means by which the roots of plants can tap into moisture, and it varies widely between types of soil, between sites, and seasonally. The water table will be closer to the soil surface in low-lying areas and deeper down on the tops of hills, but even here the water will usually be within the reach of plant roots. This is because it is held in the soil by a combination of surface tension around the soil particles and capillary action.

These effects can be lost in a raised bed, particularly if it is built above a very free-draining, pre-existing soil or if too much drainage matter is put in the base of the bed. And without access to the water table, plant roots will struggle to find their own moisture and will rely on the grower to provide for all their needs during dry weather.

Benefits for the environment

The creation of raised beds containing good-quality, well-managed soil suitable for growing plants can have positive benefits for the wider environment as well as the plants themselves.

Using recycled materials, like these pallets, to build raised beds makes good use of the Earth's resources.

While it might not be immediately obvious, the wealth of life underground is directly influenced by the levels of organic matter, minerals, and nutrients in the soil – in much the same way as plants are. And as the whole of life on the planet is interdependent, human beings are ultimately both part of this and affected by it.

As we've already seen over the preceding pages, the good-quality soil in raised beds supports healthy, productive plants. And concentrating productive growing in particular – vegetables, fruit, and cut flowers – into beds of well-maintained soil, allows other parts of our gardens and growing spaces to be left to low-intensity gardening, which can include plants that are beneficial to wildlife. But it is important to remember that all plants provide the means by which the soil is improved and life is breathed into it.

At the soil surface, and below it, this life includes bacteria, algae, fungi, worms, insects, ants, and even types of small mammal. These all play a part in processing and decomposing once-living plant material, as well as their own remains and those of surface-dwelling animals, recycling the nutrients that come from carbon-based life.

Such recycling by natural processes is inherently more rapid close to the soil surface where oxygen-containing air can penetrate, and where there is alternate wetting and drying due to rainfall or regular watering. At greater depths, usually more than 20cm (8in), soil retains more moisture and is

less aerated, which means that decomposition is slower and carbon can be retained for longer.

This benefit can only be had, however, if soil is not deeply cultivated. Digging soils in an attempt to improve them has been shown to expose the organic matter they contain to the effects of decomposition, which releases carbon dioxide back into the atmosphere. Raised-bed growing allows existing soils to be left undisturbed at depth and so hang on to their stores of carbon.

No-dig carbon store

The good-quality topsoil and organic matter mix used to fill raised beds (see page 194) optimizes growing conditions, which means the bed can be maintained with minimal disturbance and allows crops to be grown at higher densities. And adding organic matter to the surface in the form of a moisture-retentive mulch greatly reduces drying out and the resultant rapid decomposition in the soil.

This forms the basis of "no-dig" growing, where the raised beds provide easy access without the need to tread on the soil, and thus the need to dig the soil in order to relieve any resulting compaction. Maintaining an aerated, moisture-retentive soil surface with plenty of organic matter also makes planting, weeding, and harvesting easy, without much disturbance, which again would lead to drying out, decomposition, and rapid loss of carbon dioxide back into the atmosphere.

No-dig also involves leaving the roots of plants in the ground at the end of their life where they will only slowly decompose, wisely conserving their stored nutrients for use by the next set of plants or other soil organisms. This cuts down on the use of fertilizers, not only making obvious cost savings for the grower, but also reducing the environmental impacts that come from using energy to extract minerals or manufacture artificial compounds.

In addition, leaving soil undisturbed to develop a natural layered structure will maintain moisture and nutrients to a greater depth and encourage plant

roots to go down in search of these. And it is in the deep roots where there is lots of potential to lock away carbon for tens if not hundreds of years, for here, with less exposure to air, the woody material rots down very slowly, if at all.

Water where it can be used

This combination of no-dig and plentiful organic matter in a raised bed is also helpful when it comes to making wise use of water. Not only does the organic content of the soil act as a sponge to hold on to moisture and maintain a good structure for it to soak into, but the deep rooting of plants also opens up channels down which water can drain.

Rainwater will thus be able to percolate to a great depth where any excess can soak in and act as a moisture reservoir for the plants, rather than staying at the surface where it is likely to evaporate during hot, dry weather.

The soil, which provides plants with the support, moisture, and nutrients they need, also takes back their fallen leaves and other remains to recycle into raw ingredients for life.

Cycles of life

In nature and in the cultivated garden, plants provide the means by which carbon in the atmosphere is turned into living organisms. Their leaves and young stems take up carbon dioxide, while their roots absorb water, and in the presence of sunlight these are used to make carbohydrates or sugars through the process of photosynthesis. The resulting sugars, some of which are also synthesized into proteins and even simple fats by the plants, form an essential source of nutrition for the organisms that feed on them, and which may in turn be eaten, and so on through the food chain.

Ultimately, however, the soil that provides for the start of life also caters for its end. It is here that decomposition occurs of once-living material, so that it can be recycled into the basic building blocks for new life, whether it be plants, wildlife, or humanity.

Not only does this benefit the plants, but it also provides moisture for soil organisms and helps to prevent organic matter from drying out and decomposing rapidly. But there are wider environmental benefits to be had, too.

Regularly topping up raised beds with organic matter will maintain their natural moisture-holding capacity and reduce the need for supplementary watering. This will conserve rain-tank stores for when they are most needed, and ideally do away with any requirement to use mains water. Supplying this to homes uses lots of energy and chemicals in its treatment, so not using it for garden purposes results in big benefits to the environment.

Gardening in a changing climate

The very act of gardening is about managing the growing environment for plants and trying to minimize the extreme conditions that may adversely affect their growth. As our planet heats up as a consequence of increasing greenhouse gases, extreme weather events become more common, putting pressure on the soil, the plants, the wildlife, and the environment. It is perhaps periods of heat and drought that put the biggest strain on gardening and growing.

There can be no doubt that the adage of "right plant, right place" is sensible for any plot, but raised beds can help gardeners cultivate plants in a well-managed and environmentally sensitive way.

Using topsoil from your own garden mixed with home-composted organic matter creates a sustainable growing medium for beds and containers.

Benefits to urban environments

Utilizing roofs and balconies as growing spaces is a great way to grow when there is no access to open ground, and it also helps to insulate buildings from extremes of temperature. Green roofs and green walls can be used to clothe solid structures in plants, which trap air between their leaves to minimize the heating effects of the sun. But raised beds on roofs provide the additional benefit of being filled with a soil mixture that acts as a very efficient insulator. This means that it will heat up and cool down more slowly than a bare roof.

The benefits of this to the building's occupants are considerable, not only making their home more comfortable, but saving them money on energy costs for heating and cooling, too. This in turn reduces the cost to the environment, particularly when that energy comes from fossil fuels.

In urban environments especially, clothing buildings in this way has been shown to moderate temperatures at a local level, bringing benefit to the wider community.

In addition, soil-filled raised beds can be used to slow rainwater run-off. On a large scale, this may provide part of the solution to flash flooding in towns and cities.

Rooftop raised beds can help to mitigate the urban heating effects of climate change.

Benefits for garden design

One of the most useful, and arguably under-appreciated, aspects of working with raised beds is that they can help to improve the look of a garden or growing space. The visual structure they add to a plot is invaluable, and how they are used can bring lots of benefits to its design and layout.

The design function of raised beds often involves the art of "fooling the eye", by playing with the height, width, and length of the plot to create visual distractions. Wide, shallow beds will create a sense of space, making the plot feel bigger, while tall, narrow beds can make for a more regimented, if rather cluttered, look.

Equally useful from a design point of view is the way in which raised beds can be used to accentuate formality in a plot. They tend to lend themselves to straight edges and geometric shapes – such as squares, rectangles, and triangles – and so fit in well alongside patios and terraces, as well as on balconies and in courtyards.

In addition, they can be used to frame views and highlight features. Used either side of a path, door, or flight of steps, for example, raised beds can draw the attention of the eye, again creating a sense of formality. Ponds, bogs gardens, and feature planting may also benefit from the raised-bed treatment to provide attractive, eye-catching features.

All of this formal design will suit smaller, urban plots. And in some cases these will have no access to open ground on which to grow things. Small courtyards are often fully paved, while balconies and roof gardens may have enough load-bearing capacity to take the weight of additional structure, soil, and plants (see page 200). Where this is the case, deep raised beds provide opportunities for both ornamental and crop-growing spaces, all of which can enhance their overall appearance and soften the hard lines of the built environment.

Gardening on a slope

While raised beds help to make flat ground more interesting, they may also prove to be a necessity when it comes to designing a functional and attractive plot on a sloping site. Terracing – effectively beds that are raised on one side and set into the slope on the other – gives the opportunity to model the ground to incorporate either formal or informal design into a plot. Each level of terracing could be themed separately to create individual, uniquely planted sections, or layers could be linked by using the same species throughout.

Proportion and scale are always important in any aspect of design and a series of terraces will be more visually appealing than a single high wall, forming one big step down between levels.

Meanwhile, raised beds of different heights, intersecting with each other in a more modular

Terracing and raised beds can turn a steeply sloping site into a productive and accessible space for growing.

fashion, can create a funky, modern approach to garden design, whether on a slope or flat ground. This also gives the opportunity to devote space to raised pools, elevated seating areas, flights of steps, and other eye-catching features.

In addition, designing different groupings of raised beds, filled with distinct soil mixes, will allow disparate types of plants to be grown immediately alongside one another for unusual plant combinations and associations that would not otherwise be possible. This might be moisture lovers adjacent to drought-tolerant species, or types that benefit from alkaline soil next to those that require acidic conditions.

Organized growing space

When it comes to growing crops – whether it be vegetables, fruit, or cut flowers – raised beds are indispensable for both containing and organizing areas for cultivation. As we've already seen, creating specifically tailored soil mixtures for particular types of plants is made easier by containing them in raised beds, which have the added advantage of retaining the soil and preventing it from spreading into the surrounding area.

In addition, by making a series of same-sized raised beds, it is easy to organize growing, sowing, and harvesting in productive plots. This is particularly useful when crop rotation is being

These large growing cubes create a strong rhythm along the path and help to enclose the seating area behind them.

practised, where particular vegetables are grouped together according to their soil structure and nutrient requirements (see page 55 for more details). The number of years over which the rotation takes place – usually three, four, or five years – will dictate the number of beds needed of the same size, as each year the grower will need to accommodate the same area of crops from each group.

Such regular beds may also be arranged in attractive patterns; four beds in a simple two-by-two block would be the most balanced visually. But same-sized blocks in any multiples of three, four, or five could be used to make a formal layout.

Geometric layouts of repeating square and rectangular raised beds provide coherence in a garden design, even if the planting in each one is different.

Colourfully painted, interlocking raised beds and large containers make a strong statement in a modern garden design scheme.

Improving the outlook

Not only can raised beds bring plantings up into the light to benefit their growth, but also their increased height can perform the valuable function of helping to screen the sometimes unattractive boundaries of a garden or growing space.

This can be particularly useful in small spaces, such as courtyards, which can often feel very enclosed. Raised beds around the edges will add their height to that of any planting, providing more opportunities to disguise and soften the hard outlines of walls and fences. And such additional height can mean that small trees and shrubs are able to provide screening from being overlooked as well as blocking out unpleasant views.

This idea can also be used in medium and large gardens to provide screening within the plot. It may be that a raised bed in front of a shed or garden helps to reduce its visual impact, softening its outlines to blend in more with the surroundings. Meanwhile in the corners of large plots, lifting the plantings by means of raised beds will mask what is often the boundary point between multiple neighbouring gardens.

Benefits for gardeners

The advantages of raised beds apply not only to the plants; they can hugely improve the working life – as well as the physical and mental health – of the gardener, too.

Better health, growth, and performance of plants must be something the majority of gardeners wish for, and there's no doubt that carefully tailoring soil in raised beds of suitable heights brings benefit to the grower of both productive and ornamental crops. This is particularly the case where the "native" or pre-existing soil conditions are poor or degraded and can't be improved.

But raised-bed cultivation brings with it a huge raft of other benefits to the gardener, not least through lifting crops and decorative plants up to a level where they can be more readily tended. One of the fundamentals of garden design is to consider the end user and the potential for circumstances to change over time. Young children, for example, enjoy working at a suitable table height, and outdoors this is no different. Raising plants up to their eye level will help them to be more engaged with growing, and make it less tiring. Meanwhile, raised beds can be fundamental to making gardening and growing easier or even possible for those with physical restrictions in adulthood and later life (see page 104 for more details).

It is important to bear in mind, however, that the ideal height to ease access is not necessarily the ideal height for the health of plants. Raising soil above the surrounding surface level will increase aeration and drainage, which can lead to plants roots drying out more rapidly and soil nutrients washing away. And this, in turn, invariably results in the need for more watering and fertilizer application. Thus, it is crucial to balance the benefits of raising beds for access against the needs of the plants that will be grown in them.

Clearly, where access for the gardener is a prime consideration, then tall raised beds – 70–90cm (2¼–3ft) in height – are beneficial, with the caveat that it is likely to take more effort to keep the soil and the plants in good condition. And where the

Improving the soil conditions in raised beds can help optimize the performance of ornamental plants for a colourful display.

Accessible growing beds allow inclusivity and bring people together to garden.

health and performance of plants is key, then the ideal raised-bed height may only need to be 20–30cm (8–12in) to overcome poor soils, without going to the considerable expense or trouble of unnecessarily tall structures.

Benefits to garden practice

The compartmentalization of raised beds into growing spaces can help to make practical aspects of gardening and growing more convenient. Bringing the soil and plants up to a level where they can be seen more easily has the added advantage of enabling close inspection for signs of stress or pest and disease infestation. Meanwhile, weeds or undesired plants are more likely to be noticed. In all these cases, early identification of problems allows them to be dealt with before they get out of hand.

This is particularly important in the case of weeds, as when they are small they can be dispatched using a hoe or easily pulled out without disturbing the soil surface. Once established,

deep-rooted perennial weeds will require forking or digging out, which will open up the soil structure to drying out and more rapid decomposition.

Other aspects of practical maintenance can be made more onerous, however, if very tall raised beds are made. Lifting up full watering cans or buckets of mulch to use on the soil surface can be both awkward and heavy work. In addition, the use of standard garden tools such as spades, forks, hoes, and rakes will be made difficult, without climbing up onto the surface of the bed itself.

When it comes to planting, raised beds do benefit the gardener. Filled with a good-quality topsoil and organic-matter mix, hand planting with a trowel takes very little effort, particularly if the bed is narrow enough to lean in from each side without treading on the soil. The only exceptions to this are trees, large shrubs, and fruit bushes, which are impossible to plant without climbing up onto the surface of the bed itself. Meanwhile, short-growing crops are easy to harvest from raised beds, too; however, taller crops such as climbing beans, sweetcorn, and tree fruit may be too lofty to reach given the additional height.

Concentrated effort

Making the best use of space is a prime consideration for both productive and ornamental growing, and never more so than where that space is at a premium in a small garden, courtyard, or balcony. Raised beds, filled with a good-quality topsoil and organic-matter mixture, will also allow the gardener to concentrate their efforts into a limited area within the overall plot, the edges of the bed providing a frame within which to plant. This can be particularly useful for "new" gardeners, to whom a whole garden might be daunting. Equally, someone who is finding maintenance too much could usefully benefit from putting all their effort into a few raised beds and gravelling or turfing the rest of the area to make it easier to care for.

With soil improvement and maintenance directed into the raised beds, rather than diluted over a bigger area, productivity will be increased. This can be particularly useful for vegetable or cut-flower growing, where crops can be grown at closer spacings than in a wider garden.

A useful knock-on effect of growing in the limited and constrained space of raised beds is that there can be a number of psychological benefits, too. It can help the grower to feel on top of their gardening, rather than overwhelmed, for whatever reason. Not only that, but seeing plants growing well in good soil will also promote a sense of wellbeing and encourage more effort in the person who is tending them.

Then there is the feeling of security that comes from knowing you can monitor what goes into the soil your raised beds contain. This in turn dictates what the plants and wildlife feed on, and what eventually goes into the wider environment. And, of course, because all of life depends on the soil, it dictates what finds its way into the human food chain and ultimately into our bodies.

Creating a simple layout of beds for crop growing makes access and maintenance convenient.

Early pickings of leafy salads help to reduce household bills and cut out food miles.

Early crops to harvest

The improved soil and growing conditions created by well-designed and well-sited raised beds, filled with good-quality soil, has a huge benefit to the grower by often encouraging growth earlier in the season. In the case of crop plants, it can mean growth being ahead by two to four weeks in cool temperate climates. It may allow cropping to continue by a similar duration at the end of the season, too. And, of course, earlier and later cropping helps saves money on food bills and may allow an improved revenue stream where produce is being sold.

This comes about through the better aeration and drainage that occurs in the raised-up soil, preventing the plant roots from sitting in cold, waterlogged soil and allowing warm air to percolate into the soil surface on sunny spring days.

In addition, the sides of the raised bed that are presented to the sun will heat up and conduct some of this warmth into the soil. More warming benefit can be gained from the sun's energy if the raised bed is built so that the finished soil surface slopes towards the Equator: to the south in the northern hemisphere, and to the north in the southern hemisphere. In middle latitudes (North America and Northern Europe), this only need be in the region of a 7–10-degree slope.

Warm the soil early in the season by covering the surface with recycled black polythene or hessian-backed carpet for six weeks prior to sowing or planting.

Different raised bed heights for different plantings

When tailoring the height of raised beds, take into account the reason for making them, the use to which they will be put, and the gardener who will be using them. In each of the following cases, the standard width of the bed should be 1.2 metres (4ft), which allows the gardener to lean in 60cm (24in) from each side of the bed. Retaining beds may be wider or narrower than this depending on circumstances. Overall bed length may be determined by ease of access, available space, and overall design.

Capillary moisture level

Water moves up through the soil by "gravity-defying" capillary action. In tall, narrow beds well above the surrounding soil, there may not be enough moisture conveyed up to the surface by capillarity. It is at its most effective in shallow beds or in fine soil with high levels of organic matter. The blue line in the following diagrams indicates a rough estimation of the "height" moisture can easily reach in each bed during average conditions.

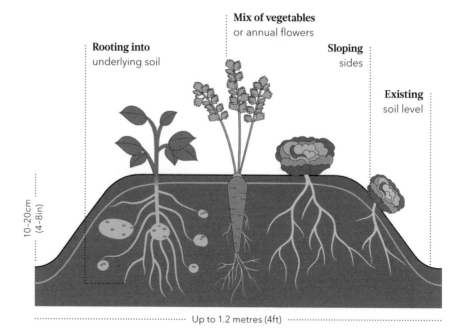

Mix of vegetables
or annual flowers

Rooting into
underlying soil

Sloping
sides

Existing
soil level

10–20cm
(4–8in)

···· Up to 1.2 metres (4ft) ····

Mounded beds

This method simply involves mounding up the soil to create a flat "table" surface to grow on. Edges can be retained and kept neat using boards, if preferred. These are the simplest form of raised bed, which allow the surface of the soil to be improved with mulches of well-rotted organic matter and retained for growing in. An easy way to increase depth on pre-existing good soil, they are useful for veg and cut-flower crops. They can also be used when creating new beds and borders in previously grass areas. These beds maintain the character and good moisture connections of the underlying natural soil. They are also useful on heavy, waterlogged soils where the mounding helps to provide a good-quality growing medium, but at the same time shed excess moisture.

Shallow beds

A widely used method of building up the depth of topsoil and organizing an area for growing. Retained edges hold the topsoil in place. A good-quality topsoil (loam) and organic-matter mix is used to fill them, usually on top of pre-existing soil. This basic adaptation of a mounded bed lifts the rooting area to allow for better drainage – particularly useful on heavy, waterlogged soils. It also enables plant roots to tap into moisture in the underlying soil, which tends to dictate the character of the raised-bed soil (i.e. sandy, chalky, clay, acidic). Suitable for veg, fruit, and flower crops.

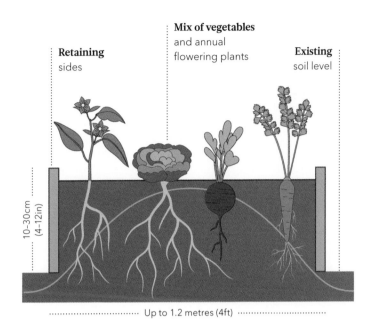

Retaining sides

Mix of vegetables and annual flowering plants

Existing soil level

10–30cm (4–12in)

Up to 1.2 metres (4ft)

Underlying soil

Mix of shrubs, flowering plants, vegetables, fruit bushes, and trees

Retaining sides

30–70cm (12in–28in)

Up to 1.2 metres (4ft)

Deep beds

Suitable for building on a solid surface where the extra depth creates a sustainable, moisture-retentive reservoir for all but the largest shrubs and trees. Can also be created on top of pre-existing soil to improve growing conditions on rubbly or very poor ground. Additional depth allows the bed to be lined and filled with specialist soil/compost mixtures to suit specific plants. Also suitable for creating garden beds for children. May be used to form terraces on shallow slopes. A greater depth of soil will result in free-drainage and there will be less connection with any underlying soil in terms of moisture and access to nutrients, with the exception of deep-rooting trees and shrubs.

Easy-access beds

These can be tailored to specific heights, for standing, seated, or wheelchair access. The bottom half is usually filled with topsoil and then filled up with a topsoil/organic-matter mix. Soil can be tailored to suit specific plants. Beds can be built on a solid base, and may be incorporated into retaining walls or on sloping ground.

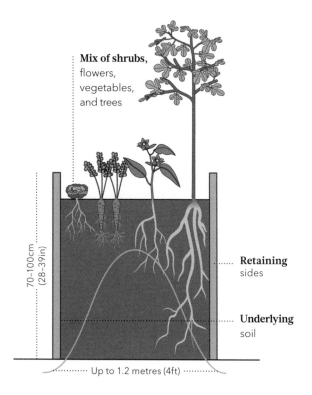

Mix of shrubs, flowers, vegetables, and trees

Retaining sides

Underlying soil

70–100cm (28–39in)

Up to 1.2 metres (4ft)

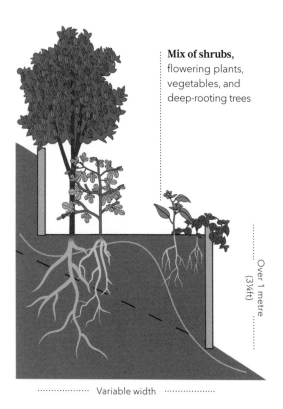

Mix of shrubs, flowering plants, vegetables, and deep-rooting trees

Over 1 metre (3¼ft)

Variable width

Retaining beds

Useful for sloping sites and to retain banks of earth. Can be built on soil or a solid surface. The lower half often mixes drainage material with topsoil. The upper half needs a quality topsoil and organic-matter mix. Such tall beds can make access difficult.

Tailoring beds for accessibility

One of the most common reasons for growing in raised beds is that the working height and width can be built or adjusted to suit the grower. This might mean raising the working level up to a convenient height for those who find bending and stooping difficult or impossible, keeping the beds small for children, or lowering the height for wheelchair users. The recommended working dimensions of raised beds for various gardeners are:

- Adults (able bodied): H30–90cm (12–35in) × W1.2 metres (4ft). The height can vary to meet the needs of the plants.
- Adults (limited mobility): H1.1 metres (3½ft) × W90cm (35in)
- Wheelchair users: H60cm (24in) × W90 (35in)
- Toddlers and young children: H45cm (18in) × W60cm (24in)
- Older children: H60cm (24in) × W90cm (35in)

Healthy body, healthy mind

There are so many ways in which gardening and plant nurturing can bring benefits to our own health and wellbeing. To begin with, organizing our growing into raised-bed blocks can make it feel much more achievable and less daunting than being faced with a large expanse of flat ground.

Studies have shown that the colour green itself is good for our mental health – we are, after all, a product of the natural world and have evolved over millions of years surrounded by it. Not only that, but the mindfulness that comes from applying ourselves to simple activities, such as weeding, sowing, and watering, provides an opportunity to slow down and disengage from our busy lives or day-to-day concerns. And, of course, there is something incredibly purposeful and rewarding about nurturing living plants and watching them grow.

Growing communities

Raised beds provide lots of ways to encourage plant growing. This brings with it wide social benefits through education, nurturing, and healthcare. Whether it is to encourage the young to take up gardening or help older and less able gardeners to continue enjoying their hobby, raised beds make good sense. Here are some ways to promote growing communities with great aspirations.

• Encourage children to get involved in gardening by allowing easy access with beds built to their height. Providing young people with simple growing skills and an appreciation of the natural world fosters interests that can be carried throughout their entire lives.

• Get involved with village and neighbourhood community gardens, featuring easy-access raised beds where food and flowers can be grown. In turn this builds social cohesion by encouraging people to work alongside one another. Projects can involve opportunities to work together in the planning, construction, planting, management, and maintenance of community raised beds, for the mutual benefit of everyone involved.

Growing food and flowers in raised beds provides a great focus for gardening with children.

• Public and private provision of raised beds allows ideal growing conditions for plants, which can be used to share knowledge between individuals and within groups. Training and tutelage in all aspects of soil management and the cultivation of plants builds wide community knowledge and practical skills, which can be passed through the generations. This also encourages horticulture and growing skills to be valued in society.

• Raised-bed garden schemes in hospitals, hospices, nursing homes, and sheltered accommodation can provide growing spaces to nurture people and their loved ones through times of illness. Lifting planting up to a higher level allows differently abled people and wheelchair users to appreciate the beauty of plants and nature at close quarters.

Raised bed pros and cons

While there are some very positive advantages to growing in raised beds, it is important to remember that they are not always essential.

Garden design and function, the quality and availability of good growing conditions, and the requirements of plants, as well as your own physical ability, all need to be considered before choosing whether or not to grow in this way.

The process of planning, designing, and building raised beds takes time and costs money, so it is important to consider whether they will bring you sufficient benefits. It is crucial to look at the pre-existing soil and growing conditions as plants may do just as well – in some cases, better – without raising the growing height.

In addition, raising soil heights in tall bed structures can reduce access for garden wildlife, in particular species like frogs, toads, and hedgehogs. Meanwhile, soil drainage can be impeded in adjacent parts of the garden where foundations are built to support raised-bed structures. It is important to note, too, that creating deeply filled beds over the roots of existing trees can cause them to die and make them unstable.

Summarizing the benefits and limitations of raised beds is a useful way of identifying how applicable they might be to an individual gardener.

Pros

- Bring soil and plants up to an easier working height.
- Make watering and other tasks quicker to perform.
- Allow for cultivation where no border soil exists on solid paved or concrete surfaces.
- Can readily tailor soil conditions for growing particular crops and plants.
- Simple to plan growing regimes and crops with regular shaped and sized beds.
- Create a level bed surface on uneven ground.
- May be incorporated into retaining walls on sloping sites.

- When filled with a good-quality growing medium, raised beds are both moisture retentive and well aerated.
- May bring plants up into more light in certain positions.
- Growing medium can be cultivated even after heavy rain.
- No-dig system simply relies on fresh compost added to surface.
- Incorporating paths can allow easy, clean access to plants.
- Can be used to lift planting on boundaries to help screening.

Shallow raised beds on existing soil are generally best for plants. They enable the soil to be improved and retained, but still allow roots to tap into the underlying soil moisture.

Choose to create raised beds where there will be tangible benefits, rather than because you think you should.

Cons

- Soil or growing medium may dry out readily.
- Beds may necessitate increased watering.
- Some nutrients – particularly nitrogen – may be more readily washed from the soil.
- Crops can be more exposed in elevated positions.
- Construction costs of large-scale structures or complexes of raised beds.
- Maintenance of raised-bed structures, depending on materials used in construction.
- Large quantities of soil and compost required to fill bed.
- Additional space required for construction of large beds.
- Visual impact of large beds on the look of the plot.

- Small beds can end up looking fussy and messy.
- Provision for paths between beds can waste space.
- Planting larger specimens can be difficult on high beds.
- Access to tall cropping plants may be awkward on tall beds.
- Potential to cover up pre-existing good-quality soil in the ground.
- May not be necessary to grow successful plants.
- Drainage of other areas of the garden may be impeded by bed construction.
- Raising soil heights over tree roots can seriously affect their health and stability.

Tall raised beds can create more work by being free-drained. This can mean that the plants dry out more readily in hot weather and so need more regular watering.

Concepts in raised beds

Following thousands of years of historical use and refinement, gardeners and growers around the world have developed ways of creating and maintaining raised beds in response to the unique soil and climate conditions that prevail in their area.

The benefits to plants of improving the soil to suit the specific conditions of a particular site remain one of the fundamental reasons for creating raised beds for growing. These soil and climate conditions vary not only on the large scale – from continent to continent, and from country to country – but also on a local scale, both regionally and even from one side of a mountain or valley to the other.

In areas of high rainfall, for example, deep beds of free-draining soil can overcome waterlogging, while in hot and dry places shallow beds of moisture-retentive soil will hold on to much-needed water for plant roots. Meanwhile at a local level,

deep beds may be of great benefit on hilltops and slopes exposed to the full force of the sun, or indeed slopes orientated away from the sun.

And while raised-bed styles and methods of creating them vary in different parts of the world, the basic principles remain the same.

Simple mound beds

The most common method of improving the soil and increasing the rooting depth for plants is to simply mound the existing soil into strips or beds. Organic matter can then be either mixed into the soil or applied as a mulch to the surface. The edges of the mounds are sloped or "chamfered" to help maintain the soil in position and so as to make the top surface of the bed level. The soil in a mound bed is obviously an upwards extension of the underlying soil, which allows plants to access moisture and nutrients from it as required.

This technique is used by farmers and growers in many parts of the world for growing crops, and is particularly useful on heavy or waterlogged ground. In Germany, the historic system of *Hügelkultur* involves making mounded beds of soil over piles

Mounded *Hügelkultur* beds provide a free-draining root run, but still allow plants to tap into underlying moisture.

Hügelkultur

Originally built as a free-standing mound, this technique involves creating layers of material that will retain moisture and decompose to release nutrients. This method can be adapted to use as filling for a raised bed with side walls. It helps to save money on the cost of topsoil to fill the bed.

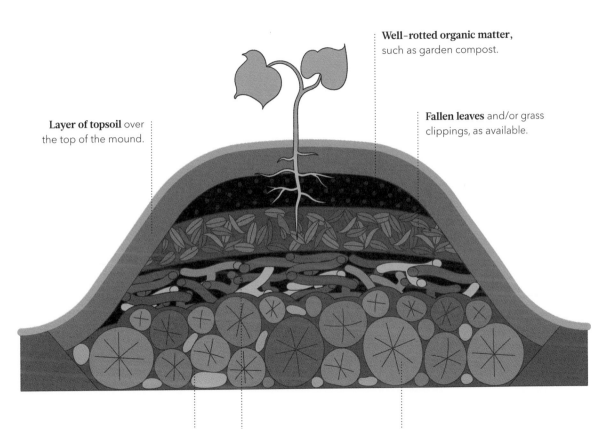

Well-rotted organic matter, such as garden compost.

Layer of topsoil over the top of the mound.

Fallen leaves and/or grass clippings, as available.

Topsoil dug out to accommodate the logs and boulder layer, and retained for covering the top of the mound.

Layer of woody twigs and short sections of thin branches.

Logs, tree-trunk sections, and large stones or boulders.

Straw bales

Popular as a way to improve soil by adding organic matter, straw bales can be used to create short-term raised beds. Well-soaked before planting, they provide a moisture-retentive root run for plants, and will decompose to create valuable organic matter for subsequent years.

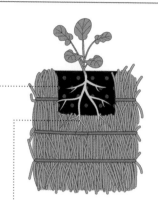

Planting pocket in the top of the bale is filled with soil. It can extend a quarter or third of the bale's depth.

Plant roots growing into the planting pocket and then down between the straws to find moisture.

Quick-maturing summer crops can produce a harvest before the straw bale disintegrates at the end of the growing season.

Optional trellis allows for climbing beans, which take nitrogen from the atmosphere into their roots, adding vital nutrients to the soil.

Straw bale is laid on its side so that the ends of the straws point upwards.

Bale twine holding the straws together.

Round bales can be used to grow wildflowers from seed for a single season while the straw decomposes. The flowers will provide nectar and pollen for insects.

of brushwood, logs, and stones, all of which provide moisture-retentive pockets, which the roots of plants can grow into. And, as all the organic components of such piles decomposes, they release nutrients for the plants to use.

An adaptation of this is the technique of "straw-bale growing", which has been used for generations in the United States, and which is now used around the world to improve soil conditions for crops (see page 188). It involves piling soil and organic matter into holes made in a pre-soaked straw bale laid on its side. Seeds and seedlings are then planted into this, where their roots grow down into the moist straw, which, as it decomposes, releases nutrients for the plants to use. By the end of the growing season the bale will have rotted down to form a mound of compost, which can then be added to each season by successive straw bales.

The sloping edges of all mounded beds are usually firmed in place with the back of a spade or the heel of a boot, to prevent the soil from washing away. They can also be turfed with grass for a more robust solution. Alternatively, the slope can be sown with a close-growing, leafy crop such as rocket or salad leaves, which will cover the soil while providing a useable harvest.

Mounded beds can be used for ornamental plants, too – most usefully for cut flowers, but also to create beds in grassed areas for mixed plantings of trees, shrubs, and herbaceous plants.

Small-space growing

In the United States, the concept of "square-foot gardening" has encouraged productive crop growing in the smallest of urban plots using a shallow timber raised bed measuring $3ft^2$. This is divided using string into $1ft^2$ patches, each of which is sown with a different successional crop. Once each crop is harvested, it is re-sown or planted to maintain a steady stream of pickings through the growing season. The metric system of "square-metre growing" has readily evolved from this in the UK, Europe, and other parts of the world (see page 154).

A keyhole bed in Rwanda, where organic matter is used to grow sustainably in a climate where soil can be quickly exhausted by intensive cultivation.

Retained or containerized raised beds

Perhaps more familiar to gardeners and allotment growers are raised beds that have some form of retaining wall built around them. These have, in part, evolved from making walls to retain soil and create terraces on sloping ground – effectively a one-sided raised bed.

On flat ground, a retaining structure that is built to contain soil or a growing medium helps to prevent it from washing away. The South American Maya people still use techniques that have been passed down through the generations to make simple, retained beds called "eras", which are little more than raised mound beds held in place around the edges with large stones.

In Africa, the more modern concept of "keyhole gardens" (see opposite) has become a popular way of enabling people on the fringes of towns and cities to grow food on modest plots. The supporting sides of these raised beds are usually made from corrugated metal sheets or stone, and circular in form. They also incorporate a narrow wedge cut into the circle to allow access to the centre of the bed. Here a compost heap or large bucket is used to recycle kitchen and leafy waste to make nutrient-rich compost that can be scraped out to enrich the soil in the rest of the bed where crops are grown. The overall structure resembles a keyhole, accounting for the name.

As we've already seen on page 36, the heights of such raised beds don't need to be very tall to improve soil depth and quality when they are built over pre-existing soil. Meanwhile, taller raised beds may be made for ease of access, as an overall garden design feature, or to provide a realistic depth of soil when building on a solid base. In the case of the latter – such as on a patio, balcony, or roof garden – this effectively creates a large container, which disconnects the bed from the underlying soil, making it more dependent on the gardener for the provision of moisture, drainage, and nutrients.

African keyhole bed

This circular bed design has become widely used in Africa and incorporates a compost bin at its centre so that essential organic matter can be recycled and used to maintain the soil. The notch in the design allows easy access to the composter.

Central bin for composting organic matter waste.

Leafy remains of plants used to make compost to enrich soil.

Soil maintained by raking out compost from the centre across the surface of the bed.

Supporting sides can be made of stone, as well as brick, timber, or tin.

Rubble and twiggy branches provide some of the fill to the base of the bed, providing moisture retention and drainage.

Elevated "table" beds, like these *canché* in the Amazon rainforest in Peru, are good for human access, and they also help discourage pest species from accessing crops.

Elevated raised beds

Lifting a growing bed entirely off the ground in some form of trough raised on legs creates the ultimate in containerized raised beds. This requires the plants to be dependent for their needs on the grower. While they can be constructed by an able DIY enthusiast, many types of small, off-the-shelf elevated or "table" beds are available to buy (see page 142).

Again, the South American Maya build raised table beds, or *canché*, using hollowed tree trunks and bark to form containers supported on legs made from thick branches. This raises the crop plants above the height where animals might graze on their leaves and roots.

Meanwhile in the rainforests of Brazil and South Asia, floating raised beds are created by filling hollowed tree trunks and canoes with soil and crop plants. These are then tethered to trees or rocks so that they can float, ark-like, at times of high rainfall and flood, before grounding out when the river levels drop.

The most elevated of all raised beds are green roofs (see page 132) and living walls (see page 133). The former usually consist of a shallow depth of free-draining growing medium for the cultivation of drought-tolerant plants. Meanwhile, living walls are formed of small planting recesses to contain compost and plants.

The creation of large containers for green roofs and living walls has opened up huge possibilities for covering our modern buildings with living plant material to help mitigate the effects of climate change. Many cities around the world are seeing skyscrapers, apartment blocks, and individual houses being built with gardens, green walls, and even forests incorporated into their design.

The foliage of these plantings not only helps to moderate extremes of heat and cold in our built environments, but also provides valuable humidity, absorbs particulate pollution, and offers habitat for wildlife. Add to that the benefits that the colour green has on people's mental health, and raised-bed growing looks set to become an even more important element in our lives.

Vertical growing systems optimize space and help limit extremes of temperature in urban environments.

What could you grow?

Deciding what to grow

Whether you are growing your own food, making perfect spaces for your favourite blooms, building a stylish pond, or helping pollinators and wildlife, raised beds offer a creative way to make the most of your outdoor – and even indoor – growing space, whatever its size.

Get inspired

Inspiration is easy to come by with raised beds, as you can grow pretty much anything in this sort of structure. In this section we'll look at some of the ways you can use them to improve the growing conditions for your plants. As with any aspect of design, it's all about getting ideas and then tailoring them to suit your own plot.

Raised beds could help to improve your productivity for growing your own vegetables and salad crops, fruit, and even herbs. With them

Changing levels allows flowering plants to be appreciated more fully.

Introducing our Raised Bed Heroes

To help you gather inspiration for what you might grow in a raised bed, we have called upon some of the top gardening influencers from around the world – our Raised Bed Heroes - to share their ideas for what to plant and their own experiences of "elevated growing".

Over the course of the next two chapters you will discover a series of simple yet inspired planting plans created by our Heroes and themed around their particular passions, from cut flowers

to cocktail herbs. Each easy-to-follow plan includes an explanation of the design and a planting sketch to help with positioning, together with a list of the featured plants and numbers needed. Alongside the planting plan, each Hero also explains why they love growing in raised beds, and shares a few nuggets of gardening wisdom to help your plants thrive.

We hope these features will open your eyes to the possibilities and inspire your own creations.

Herbs make perfect subjects for raised-bed growing and this multi-layer arrangement looks stylish, too.

Raised beds make tending vegetable crops easier.

prominently in view you'll be able to check when they're ready to water, protect, and harvest. They can also help you organize and plan your production, as well as improve the soil for particular types of crops. As any serious food grower will tell you that replacing organic matter and nutrients used up by the plants (and effectively removed at harvest time) is crucial for success.

In a similar way, raised beds make good sense when it comes to growing ornamental plants. Getting the soil in good condition to suit the specific types of plants you want to grow is made easier in what is fundamentally an empty box. Whether it is gritty soil for alpines, acid soil for ericaceous plants, moisture-retentive rich soil for cut flowers and bedding displays, or free-draining conditions for wildflowers and nectar-rich flowers, tailored soil mixes can be used for filling raised beds to get plants off to the best start.

And don't forget to think creatively about other things that could go in the box. Ponds, bog gardens, lawns, and extra-special collections of plants all have raised-bed potential. You can even engineer them to help plants cope with extreme weather and the climate changes we're all facing.

Over the following pages you'll find plenty of inspiration to help you decide what to grow, with simple considerations to bear in mind before you get started…

Productive veg and salad beds

Nothing beats the taste of homegrown food, and any veg grower will tell you that getting the soil right is the key to successful and intensive cropping. Raised beds are a great way to get the best results from a whole range of different crops, and they can help take the backache out of growing, too.

Beds for easy access

Grow-your-own veg is probably how most gardeners are introduced to raised beds. While not essential to the process, they do offer a convenient way to tailor and manage soil fertility to optimize the rooting environment and get the most from a range of different crops. Simply edging vegetable growing beds with planks allows you to improve the soil by adding organic matter and retains it in place, keeping the growing area well organized and looking cared for.

The higher level of crop maintenance involved in productive growing – particularly for vegetables and salad crops – makes a good case for creating tall raised beds to reduce stooping and the effort involved in getting up and down to carry out different cultural tasks. Practically speaking, the most beneficial crops to raise in height are leafy and stem crops, such as lettuce, as well as root crops, such as carrots – all of which are low growing and require bending to sow, tend, and harvest.

By contrast, once established, fruiting vegetables such as peas or tomatoes are, for the most part, produced on taller-growing plants. Growing these in raised beds might be thought to add a physical disadvantage when it comes to installing any growing supports or harvesting.

In raised veg beds you can control the growing medium to ensure it is moisture-retentive yet free-draining, which are the ideal conditions for seasonal salad crops.

Keep it moving

While not essential in all cases, crop rotation – moving groups of vegetables to a different position from one growing season to the next – can be useful in helping to reduce the carry-over of pests and diseases. Where space allows, this might involve allocating a whole bed each to leafy crops, potatoes, roots, and fruiting vegetables, and moving them every year. In small spaces with fewer beds, crops can simply be moved to a new position each growing season. (See Chapter 5 for more on the care requirements of different plants.)

The tiniest outside spaces can provide the opportunity for growing in raised beds. This could be a tall, narrow bed built along the brightest side of a small courtyard or balcony, and filled with seasonal crops. Alternatively, a 1 metre^2 (3¼ft^2) free-standing bed can be cropped intensively using easy, quick-growing veg and salads.

Raising up essential culinary herbs makes regular picking easy and convenient.

Easy crops for raised beds

Try these quick-growing, seasonal crops, which are easy to grow from seed and will give you plenty of fresh, healthy pickings. They'll be full of flavour and sweetness, plus you'll be cutting down drastically on food miles. Plan for a continuity of crops by sowing small batches of seed successively (every three to four weeks in the growing season).

Leafy salads
Lettuce, lamb's lettuce, rocket, salad leaves, land cress, spring onions

Leafy veg
Spinach, pak choi, Swiss and rainbow chard, leaf beet, kale

Root crops
Carrots, beetroot, turnips, garlic, shallots, fennel, radishes

Fruiting crops
Bush and French beans, climbing and runner beans, sweetcorn (maize), peas, tomatoes

Bumper fruit cropping

Dessert fruits make a low-maintenance and perennial cropping addition to any plot. And whether you choose cordon-trained apples or strawberries, raised beds will ensure that you maximize your return.

Permanent plantings
of fruit bushes and trees
will crop every year.

For maximum sweetness

One of the easiest ways to enjoy a bumper harvest from your growing space is to plant dessert fruits. In temperate climates these are usually hardy perennials that will grow year after year, yielding delicious crops without the intensive care required for most veg. In warmer climates, the fruit bowl can be reliably augmented by planting citrus as well as subtropical and annual fruit crops.

Raised beds are a good option for growing the more compact forms of fruit. You can tailor the soil to be well aerated and moisture retentive by the yearly addition of an organic mulch. This will also provide the plants with most of the nutrients they need. And, in the case of blueberries and other fruits that require lime-free conditions, an ericaceous soil mix can be used to fill the bed.

Deep beds will provide good conditions for bush fruit (such as currants and gooseberries) and top fruit (apples, pears, plums, etc.), although the latter would benefit from being grafted onto growth-restricting rootstocks.

And with corner posts installed in the beds, fruit nets can be easily deployed to protect your assets from pests in a limited space.

Blueberries benefit from being grown in raised beds as their need for acidic soil can be met and they can be easily netted to protect against hungry birds.

Aim high for strawberries

The sweetness and flavour of homegrown strawberries is unbeatable, but you won't be the only one after the juicy fruits. They're a particular favourite of slugs and snails, as well as mice and a number of different bird species. In moist seasons you may also find the berries marred by grey mould before you get the chance to pick them.

Raised-bed growing is regularly used by commercial growers to lift the plants above normal ground level, and hopefully away from marauding molluscs and mice. In addition, raising the strawberry crop above other plants will ensure better air circulation to limit mould growth, as well as exposing the fruit to more sun for better ripening.

You could try growing strawberries in their own, exclusive bed or using them as edge planting around other fruit, veg, or even ornamentals.

Six of the best fruit crops

Often in need of tailored growing conditions, fruits are ideal for raised beds. Give them the soil and situation they require and they will reward you with a bumper crop.

Blueberries
Perfect for growing in raised beds as the soil can be tailored to suit the lime-free conditions they require. Grow in a position that gets sun for at least half the day. Woody perennial.

Cranberries
Requiring a lime-free soil, cranberries suit raised-bed cultivation with plenty of organic matter in the growing mix to retain moisture. Can be grown under other plants in semi-shade. Woody perennial.

Gooseberries
These tough, bumper-cropping fruits benefit from growing in a raised bed and open situation where they will get good air circulation. This will help prevent mildew disease. Woody perennial.

Raspberries
These do best in a position with sun for part of the day, or in dappled shade. Choose a mix of both summer- and autumn-fruiting varieties for a long season of pickings. Woody perennial.

Strawberries
Will benefit from cultivation in a raised bed to lift the fruit above the ground. This will help to keep plants dry and reduce the risk of grey mould fungus and slug damage. Herbaceous perennial.

Tomatoes
This salad fruit will do well in a raised bed, in a sunny position. Choose tomato-blight-resistant varieties when growing outdoors in moist, temperate climates. Tender perennial.

Tailor-made for healthy herbs

Growing culinary herbs is one of the most popular gateways into gardening. These resilient plants do best if grown tough, without lots of additional nutrients, to accentuate their piquancy and flavour, and raised beds can be filled with suitable soil recipes for the best results.

Recreating natural habitats

Historically herbs have played a fundamental part in human health and nutrition, while at the same time making our food more palatable. The plants we grow in our plots today come from all round the world; growing enough of these plants to have plentiful pickings to use in cooking should be the main aim, so recreating something akin to the growing conditions in their native habitat is the key to success.

For most Mediterranean herbs, such as thyme or rosemary, a seasonally hot climate and free-draining soil that's low in nutrients will concentrate the natural aromatic oils and compounds in the foliage that give these plants their distinctive taste. Meanwhile, those that have their origins in subtropical and tropical climates, such as lemongrass, turmeric, or ginger, will benefit from more moisture, both in the soil at the roots and in the atmosphere.

Plant up a herb pyramid

This diagram groups together herbs with similar growing needs, from those that love free-draining soil and fare well in drought, to those that need constant moisture.

THYME
OREGANO
MARJORAM
SAVORY
DILL
SAGE

Drought-tolerant herbs suitable for growing in the top tier of a herb pyramid

ROSEMARY
FENNEL
CORIANDER
TARRAGON
BASIL
BAY

Versatile herbs that enjoy relatively moist but still free-draining conditions

LEMONGRASS
CHERVIL
PARSLEY
CHIVES
LOVAGE
ANGELICA
MINT

Moisture-loving herbs suitable for growing at the base of a herb pyramid

Tiered planting

Such plant preferences can be well catered for by grouping herbs that require similar conditions into their own raised bed filled with a suitable soil mixture. And by creating a multi-layer arrangement of beds set up on at least three levels, you can cater for the needs of the different herb types. Those that benefit from the driest soil and most intense heat can be planted in the topmost layer, where excess water will quickly drain away from their roots and into the next layer down. Here, plants that benefit from a little more moisture will have longer to absorb what they need. Meanwhile, at the lowest level, water will collect as it soaks down from the top to provide a moisture-retentive and cool root run.

Such a "herb tower" can be created at different sizes and dimensions to suit the available space and quantities of pickings required (see page 162). While the most obvious plan might be to create a regular pyramid of layers in decreasing sizes, the

(Top, left to right)

Oregano Does best in full sun and free-draining soil.

Mint Loves moisture-retentive soil and copes with part shade.

Golden marjoram This pale-leaved form does best in part shade.

(Bottom, left to right)

Parsley Likes moist soil and can be grown in full sun or part shade.

Rosemary Grow in full sun and free-draining soil.

Sage Plant in full sun and free-draining soil to keep compact and flavourful.

position, size, and orientation of each section can be tailored to your own plot and requirements.

It's not only culinary herbs that'll do well with such attention to detail. This kind of soil tailoring and layering can be copied for other types of raised-bed growing – both productive and ornamental.

Grow herbs
for cocktails

Mark Diacono

I think, if push came to shove, I could happily garden using only raised beds. Everywhere I've lived, everywhere I've designed gardens, has featured them. A little work establishing a raised bed and you've overwritten any limitations in the local growing medium, and you can provide your plants with excellent drainage and warmer temperatures.

Brushing your hand over the leaves of this pelargonium will release its rose-like scent.

Mark Diacono is an award-winning food and garden writer, known for growing and cooking everything from Szechuan pepper to asparagus to Korean mint to Asian pears. Twice winner of Food Book of the Year and Garden Book of the Year, Mark has inspired a new generation of people to grow some of what they eat. He has written and photographed 13 books and was shortlisted for a James Beard Foundation award for his book *SOUR: The Magical Element That Will Transform Your Cooking*. Mark was involved in the early days of chef Hugh Fearnley-Whittingstall's organic smallholding project River Cottage, appearing in the TV series and writing three of the River Cottage Handbook series. His next book, *VEGETABLES*, is published in 2024.

What's more, you've created a defining line between your plants and the path/lawn beyond, brought structure to the garden, and – if you build the edges high and wide enough – given yourself somewhere to sit, overcoming any inability (or reluctance) to bend low to tend the plants. What's not to love?

Raised beds have taught me the importance that an agglomeration of small differences can make: the drainage, quality of substrate, and slight shift in temperature from being away from ground level mean plants and seeds get away more quickly early in the season and often withstand extreme wet or cold better than those in the ground.

Perhaps most of all, raised-bed growing suits my brain. Each bed gives me an understandable, intentional space in which to focus: this bed is for unusual root crops, that one is where I grow cut-and-come-again salads, and so on. And I find the regularity that they bring – even in a wider design of curves and flow – deeply satisfying. Experience has taught me that you should use thicker wood than you ideally want to spend money on, and that your raised bed should be taller than you'd ideally like to fill with compost, because once you've made it and enjoy what it brings, you'll want it to remain a permanent part of the garden.

A palette of flavours

At some point, the edible gardener has to decide what resources – time, money, space – they are able to commit to what they do. This almost always involves deciding whether to prioritize volume or flavour. I fall into the latter camp. Give me a space that will give me small, repeated harvests of deliciousness over a barrowful of staples any day. This raised bed exemplifies that thinking.

Full of perennial herbs that are not available in the shops, it offers a wider palette of flavours than non-gardeners enjoy. Anise hyssop (for extraordinary mojitos), ginger rosemary (for the best Tom Collins), and lemon verbena (for limoncello) are among my favourite flavours, and you can only have them if you grow them yourself. Add to that, this bed is low maintenance, pollinator friendly, and – being perennial – gives you long-lasting beauty.

Herbs for cocktails

PLANT LIST

Most of these are perennial herbs, so I would plant medium/large single plants so as to be able to harvest at least a little early on. The annual basils I would plant as small 9cm (3½in) pots.

Anise hyssop / *Agastache foeniculum*
Thai basil / *Ocimum basilicum* var. *thyrsiflora* × 3
Ginger rosemary / *Salvia rosmarinus* 'Green Ginger'
Salad burnet / *Sanguisorba minor*
Scots lovage / *Ligusticum scoticum*
Orange-scented thyme / *Thymus* 'Fragrantissimus'
Lime basil / *Ocimum* x *africanum* 'Lime' × 5
Sweet cicely / *Myrrhis odorata*
Lemon verbena / *Aloysia citrodora*
African blue basil / *Ocimum kilimandscharicum* × *basilicum* 'Dark Opal' × 6
Pineapple sage / *Salvia elegans*
Rose-scented pelargonium / *Pelargonium* 'Attar of Roses'

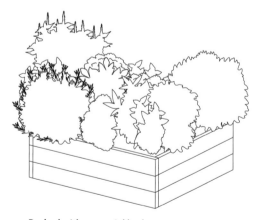

Packed with perennial herbs, this bed gives a lasting display, as well as aromatic ingredients for your favourite cocktails.

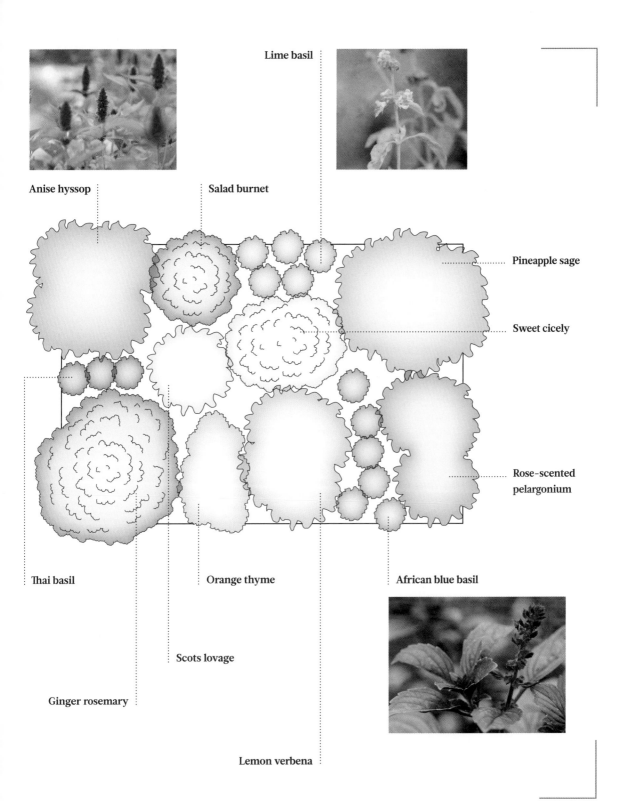

Lime basil

Anise hyssop

Salad burnet

Pineapple sage

Sweet cicely

Rose-scented
pelargonium

Thai basil

Orange thyme

African blue basil

Scots lovage

Ginger rosemary

Lemon verbena

Growing alpine plants

Free drainage and good soil aeration are fundamental to success when growing alpine plants. Creating a raised bed provides the ideal opportunity to tailor growing conditions that will suit them right down to the ground.

Adapted for drought

The soil or growing medium needed for plants varies widely according to their origins and can be very particular, none more so than for those that come from mountainous regions of the world. Here, soils are composed of a high proportion of weathered rock and there are few ready sources of organic matter available.

It can come as a surprise to find that alpine plants show lots of adaptations to drought: in summer there can be severe exposure to sun and little in the way of rain, while in winter moisture is locked up in the form of ice or snow. And with steep terrain, excess water readily drains away.

Bringing the mountain to the garden

Recreating these growing conditions in low-altitude locations with a more temperate climate and rich, deep soils can be challenging. Raised beds filled with a gritty, free-draining growing medium are ideal and are often referred to as "scree gardens". Built with shallow walls of rough rock or even finished stone, without mortar, the beds aim to recreate the montane soil conditions, while the top surface can be sloped and enhanced with rocks to create ideal planting pockets to suit the plants.

On a sloping site, an adaptation of this environment can be to build drystone retaining walls, which are then backfilled with a gritty medium to allow alpines to grow successfully. Leaving the gaps between the stone un-mortared allows young specimens to be literally "built in" to the bed's construction, where the plants can take advantage of the free-draining conditions, similar to those found on a mountain rock face.

Such structures can be made to emulate the natural conditions where these plants grow and can be successfully incorporated into a wide range of garden designs, creating either a complementary or contrasting feature.

Stepped rock gardens are a traditional form of raised bed recreating the gritty, free-draining conditions of the original mountainous habitats of alpines (far left); lifting these delicate plants into view means their intricate detail can be better appreciated (left).

Alpine plants are ideal for raised beds where you can better appreciate their often exquisitely delicate forms. Also, the special soil conditions mean that a wide range of varieties can be curated and grown with success.

Androsace (any species)
Fully frost hardy, making spreading mats of intricate foliage, speckled with small flowers in spring. All benefit from being grown in sun.

Sempervivum
With fleshy leaves and roots, sempervivums are adapted to dry soils but are frost hardy to -5°C (23°F) or lower. These plants need full sun to thrive.

Juniperus communis 'Compressa'
Slow-growing dwarf conifer. Ideal for creating height among alpines. Grows well in sun or part shade.

Saxifraga
The alpine forms of this plant are all low growing and mat forming, with dainty leaves and masses of flowers in spring. Most benefit from sun.

Gentiana septemfida
Clump forming with a low, spreading habit. Produces spectacular tube-like flowers in spring or autumn. Grow in sun or part shade.

Iris reticulata (and hybrids/varieties)
Short bulbs flowering in various colours from late winter to early spring. Foliage dies back in summer. Likes full sun.

Lewisia hybrids
Makes a rosette of fleshy leaves and clusters of blooms on short stalks in the summer. Colours vary from white to pink to apricot. Requires full sun.

Phlox subulata
Low-growing and mat-forming evergreen, covered in white, pink, or lavender blooms in late spring and early summer. Best in sun or part shade.

Daphne cneorum
Dwarf, dome-shaped shrub with evergreen foliage and clusters of scented spring flowers. Grow in sun or part shade, on well-drained soil.

Lime-free growing for ericaceous plants

Raised beds can help you overcome limitations in a range of soil conditions, most usefully for those plants that are unable to thrive and survive with lime at their roots.

Easy solutions for picky plants

Providing acidic soil for ericaceous (lime-hating) plants is made simple by using a raised bed. For gardeners who have alkaline soil and want to grow plants such as rhododendrons, azaleas, and camellias, for example, it is the only long-term option. This is also a useful solution in courtyards and on balconies, or anywhere without suitable native soil to plant into.

Conveniently, ericaceous plants have fibrous roots, which tend to grow close to the surface, rather than going down deep into the soil. This means they are well suited to growing in a contained root run. You can line the base and sides of such a raised bed to help retain the soil and organic-matter mix (see page 189), as well as to stop any alkalinity leaching in from underlying soil. Alternatively, deep raised beds can be built on top of a solid paved surface if no garden space exists.

Finding the perfect pH

Alkaline or limey soils are found over chalk and limestone rocks, as well as those that contain high levels of sodium salts. Dry soils in hot climates, and heavily polluted soils, can also prove very alkaline. It is important to remember that mains and borehole water may contain lime or other mineral salts, even if your soil is acidic or you create a raised bed filled with ericaceous soil. Such water can quickly make the soil or compost become progressively alkaline. In such cases, take care to use rainwater around ericaceous plants.

You can use a pH soil testing kit to assess your soil's relative alkalinity or acidity. For gardening purposes, acid soils are in the range of pH 3–6.5 and alkaline soils pH 7.1–8, while those around pH 6.5–7 are considered broadly neutral and suitable for a wide range of plants.

Heathers, such as these *Calluna vulgaris* varieties, need to grow in soils with a pH below 6.5 for best results.

While most plants can adapt to slight differences in soil type, ericaceous plants have evolved to grow in acidic soil and will likely die in alkaline conditions. If a pH test reveals that your garden soil is higher than pH 7 you'll need to use an acid or ericaceous soil mix for the following plants:

Summer heather (*Calluna vulgaris* and varieties)
Provides summer colour and keeps foliage all year. Compact and low growing if trimmed back after flowering. Great for bees and other insects.

Winter heather (*Erica carnea* and other varieties)
Small evergreen, needle-like leaves; abundant winter flowers on compact, low bushes, gradually spreading to form ground-covering mats.

Prickly heath (*Gaultheria mucronata* and varieties)
Dark, evergreen foliage on compact, rounded bushes; clusters of white early-summer flowers, followed in autumn and winter by large berries.

Lily-of-the-valley bush (*Pieris japonica, P. floribunda,* and other species and varieties)
Broad-leaved evergreen medium-sized bush. Clusters of bell-like flowers in late spring.

Yakushima rhododendrons (*Rhododendron yakushimanum* and varieties)
Broad, evergreen foliage, often with tan underside. Clusters of large flowers in late spring.

Deciduous azaleas (*Rhododendron luteum* and varieties)
Foliage drops in winter. Large blooms, in shades of yellow and orange, in late spring.

Autumn-flowering gentian (*Gentiana sino-ornata* and other species and varieties)
Mat-forming herbaceous plants that die back in winter. Leaves tipped with trumpet-like, intense blue flowers in autumn.

Purple gromwell (*Lithodora diffusa* and varieties)
Spreading, mat-forming evergreen with mid-green leaves. Produces dark to mid-blue, tubular flowers in early summer.

Japanese rose (*Camellia japonica* and other species and varieties)
Evergreen bushes with glossy foliage. Single- or double-petalled blooms from late autumn to late spring.

Creative habitats for pollinators

Devoting a plot to nectar-rich plants is a great way to do your bit for the environment and boost your gardening. Grow these plants in a raised bed or green roof and they'll benefit from good drainage and plenty of light.

Rich in nectar

So many of our cultivated crops and flowers rely on insects to pollinate them, and it's not just bees that do the work. A whole host of wasps, flies, beetles, and other insects provide plants with the vital service of transferring pollen from flower to flower, and in return they get a free meal to help them on their way.

Creating an all-year-round "nectar bar" of flowers will be of huge benefit to such wildlife – and, if you let loose your imagination, there are plenty of ways to use raised growing systems to optimize the growth of plants for pollinators.

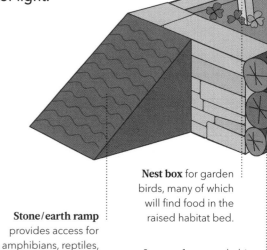

Teasels and other seedheads provide food for birds and mammals in winter.

Nest box for garden birds, many of which will find food in the raised habitat bed.

Stone/earth ramp provides access for amphibians, reptiles, and mammals.

Log stack creates habitat and the decomposing wood provides food and nesting sites.

Avoid cutting back herbaceous perennials in autumn as they provide an overwintering habitat for the eggs, chrysalises, and adults of a wide variety of insects.

Late-season asters provide plenty of nectar for a wide range of butterfly species.

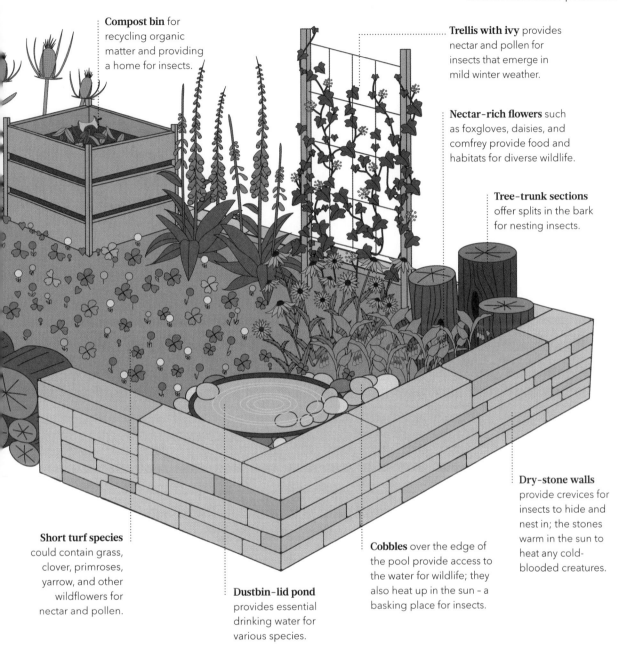

Compost bin for recycling organic matter and providing a home for insects.

Trellis with ivy provides nectar and pollen for insects that emerge in mild winter weather.

Nectar-rich flowers such as foxgloves, daisies, and comfrey provide food and habitats for diverse wildlife.

Tree-trunk sections offer splits in the bark for nesting insects.

Dry-stone walls provide crevices for insects to hide and nest in; the stones warm in the sun to heat any cold-blooded creatures.

Cobbles over the edge of the pool provide access to the water for wildlife; they also heat up in the sun - a basking place for insects.

Dustbin-lid pond provides essential drinking water for various species.

Short turf species could contain grass, clover, primroses, yarrow, and other wildflowers for nectar and pollen.

The pollen itself is high in protein and may be eaten by some insects, but in addition, lots of flowers incorporate "nectaries" at the base of the petals where nectar is produced. The sweet, sticky substance – effectively a solution of sugars made by the plant – is taken up by the roots and transported through the stems and leaves.

This is referred to as sap throughout the plant, but in the nectaries other volatile, aromatic substances may be added prior to release to form nectar, which is used to attract passing insects. High in carbohydrates (sugars), this is an important energy source for insects and other animals.

Long-season blooms

For the best results it is important to choose an open, sunny spot to grow your nectar-producing plants. This is the most likely place to promote blooming and it will help the flowers to be full of pollen and nectar. But, equally important, exposure to the sun will warm the bodies of the insects and help maintain their activity levels. Think about building the bed from stone, or at least incorporating some large stones as these will heat up in the sun, providing warm places for them to bask. And include a small pool filled with cobbles to cater for their water needs.

Local wildlife will undoubtedly benefit from native plants in your area, but many introduced and "exotic" species also produce plentiful nectar and pollen. Widening your plant choice may well extend the season of food available to pollinators and other species, while at the same time looking colourful and attractive over a long period. For this, there are masses of short-growing herbaceous perennial plants and ornamental grasses that would be suitable for cultivation in a raised bed at ground level or to form a deep green roof, with drought-resistant and prairie species particularly suitable. With careful selection, it should be possible to have flowers from late winter, through spring and summer into late autumn.

The soil-mixture fill needs to be moisture-retentive but, most importantly, free-draining to prevent the plants becoming waterlogged. It should also be fairly low in nutrients – in particular nitrogen – to limit an overabundance of foliage growth at the expense of nectar- and pollen-producing flowers. And if planning a green roof bed, remember to check the bearing weight of the roof and use a lightweight growing medium rather than heavy soil and gravel.

20 nectar-rich flowers

Snowdrops (*Galanthus* species and varieties)

Primrose (*Primula vulgaris*)

Christmas and Lenten rose (*Helleborus niger* and *H. x hybridus*)

Grape hyacinth (*Muscari* species and varieties)

Foxglove (*Digitalis purpurea*)

Bedding and lawn daisies (*Bellis perennis*)

Lavender (*Lavandula* species and varieties)

Shrubby veronica (*Hebe* species and varieties)

Butterfly bush (*Buddleja davidii* and other species)

Bee balm/wild bergamot (*Monarda didyma*)

Yarrow (*Achillea* species and varieties)

Zinnias (*Zinnia* varieties)

Cosmos (*Cosmos atrosanguineus*)

Joe-pye-weed (*Eupatorium purpureum*)

Anise hyssop (*Agastache foeniculum*)

Borage (*Borago officinalis*)

Coneflower (*Echinacea* species and varieties)

Milkweed/Butterfly weed (*Asclepias* species and varieties)

Black-eyed Susan (*Rudbeckia* species and varieties)

Golden rod (*Solidago* species and varieties)

The nectar-rich *Echinacea purpurea* will attract bees and other pollinators to your garden.

Cut-flower garden

Bringing fresh flowers indoors is a treat at any time of year, and even the smallest plot can provide space for your own cutting garden. Raised beds make planning, planting, and maintenance easy, as well as providing great soil for the best blooms.

Floral pickings from raised beds are perfect for bringing indoors for decoration.

The cutting bed

Whether it's a bouquet for a special occasion, a generous bunch for your own seasonal arrangement, or a single bloom on a bedside table for a house guest, flowers picked fresh from your plot are a luxury, but they really couldn't be easier to achieve.

Situated in a sheltered corner, with plenty of light, a raised bed helps to demark the flowers for picking. When it's filled with good soil and topped up with plenty of organic matter each season, you can pack in the plants more closely than you would in garden borders to maximize your floral crop.

Choice cuts

For best results, choose plants that produce lots of flowers, preferably over a long season. Plus, it's important to select those that have a long vase life: some simply wilt because they don't like being picked or drop their petals within a few hours. You may also want to add scented blooms to the mix to make the best room fragrancers.

Annual plants offer some of the easiest-to-grow options when it comes to cut flowers. These are sown from seed to bloom during the growing season. In temperate climates they will mostly offer summer and early-autumn flowers; sow small batches of seed at three-to-four-week intervals in spring to provide a succession of stems to cut. Hardy annuals can be sown direct outdoors where they are to flower, while half-hardy and tender types are best raised indoors, ready for planting out once all fear of frost has passed.

Spring and summer bulbs are also a great choice, although in many cases each bulb will produce only one or two flowers. However, they are relatively cheap and can be mass planted to provide plenty of pickings. The term "bulb" is used to cover true bulbs, corms, and tubers – the latter category including dahlias, which will produce masses of flowers from a single plant.

Some of the taller spring- and summer-flowering herbaceous perennials make great cut flowers, with the bonus that the plants will grow back year after year. Equally useful are some shrubs – especially those that flower in the winter when there are no annuals, bulbs, or herbaceous plants in bloom.

And it's not just flowers that are valuable for cutting; seedheads, twigs with coloured bark, and different types of foliage are also indispensable. You can use any or all of these as fillers to flowers or as a colourful display in their own right.

Top-20 flowers for a cutting bed

You'll be spoilt for choice when it comes to flowers, berries, foliage, and stems for cutting. Here is just a selection of some reliable species to provide blooms to enjoy indoors:

Daffodil - Mar-Apr (Bu)
Tulip - Apr-May (Bu)
Allium - May-Jun (Bu)
Love-in-a-mist (nigella) - May-Jul (A)
Pinks - Jun-Aug (P)
Ammi majus - Jun-Aug (A)
Cornflower - Jun-Aug (A)
Alstroemeria - Jun-Aug (P)
Lily - Jun-Sep (Bu)
Sweet pea - Jun-Sep (A)
Zinnia - Jul-Sep (A)
Gladioli - Jul-Sep (Bu)
Cosmos - Jul-Sep (A)
Dahlia - Jul-Sep (Bu)
Rudbeckia - Jul-Sep (A and P)
Michaelmas daisy - Sep-Oct (P)
Crocosmia - Aug-Oct (Bu)
Sedum - Sep-Oct (P)
Viburnum × bodnantense 'Dawn' - Oct-Mar (S)
Laurustinus - Oct-Apr (S)

P - perennial
Bu - bulb/corm/tuber
A - annual
S - shrub

Clockwise from top left:
Dwarf tulips are great for small arrangements; alliums make long-lasting cut flowers; spectacular lilies last well as cut blooms; add a touch of fire to autumn arrangements with crocosmia; cosmos are easy to grow and are good for cutting.

Seasonal centrepiece

Ever-popular bedding plants and annual flowers are easy to grow for maximum impact. Create a focal point by packing them into a raised bed, and ring the changes with new sowings and plantings to celebrate the seasons of the year.

Colour and impact

Colourful flowers are a sure-fire way to bring interest to your garden, courtyard, or balcony, and there's a strong tradition of planting seasonal displays. Spring blooms are particularly anticipated after the dark days of winter, while summer flowers provide a way of decorating your plot when you're most likely to be outdoors to enjoy it.

Bedding plants and bulbs offer some of the most floriferous options for gardeners, but it can be expensive to buy enough for an eye-catching show, and dotting a few here and there will dilute their effect. By contrast, grouping all the seasonal bedding together in a raised bed will create a strong focal point and give you the opportunity to experiment with colour contrasts and harmonies. Sited at the edge of a patio or in a sunny corner of your plot – somewhere visible – the bed can be filled with good-quality soil and topped up with well-rotted organic matter once a year. This will concentrate your funds and efforts into an achievable space. And with the plants swapped out alternately for the seasons, you'll have a colour-packed show to enjoy.

Don't forget that many bedding plants are easy to grow from seed and cuttings yourself. Start them off indoors in pots and seed trays so you have well-developed young plants to pop in the bed

Colourful winter plants make an eye-catching display in the shortest days of the year (top), while tulips and spring bedding plants welcome the longer days (bottom).

when it's time to make the seasonal change. Meanwhile, the most economical option for summer colour is to sow directly into the soil where the plants are to grow, using packets of hardy and half-hardy annuals. It couldn't be easier!

Create cut-flower beds

Anya Lautenbach

Creating a cutting garden in raised beds is a great idea. As your flowers will grow on a higher level, you'll be able to enjoy them with all your senses. You'll be closer to the beauty you grow yourself. Many low-growing plants will be at the right level for you to touch them as you walk by. Picking your flowers to create a wonderful display will be easier, too.

Colourful annuals *Salvia viridis* and *Nigella damascena* make excellent cut flowers, holding their shape and colour well.

Anya Lautenbach is a self-taught gardener with a passion for the environment and championing neurodiversity. She grew up in Poland, and after travelling for many years in Germany and the Scottish Highlands, she now lives with her husband and two sons in Buckinghamshire, UK, where her garden has blossomed through years of propagation and clever gardening tricks.

Anya's lifelong passion for propagating plants inspired her to share her knowledge with her followers across social media. There, as Anya the Garden Fairy, she provides easy-to-follow tutorials covering a range of accessible and achievable gardening techniques, and reveals tips and tricks for creating high-impact, low-cost gardens that work in harmony with nature.

Instagram: @anya_thegarden_fairy

Cutting gardens are a magnet for wildlife such as butterflies and other precious pollinators, so growing flowers in raised beds will allow you to be closer to nature. Your raised cutting garden will give you a great sense of achievement.

To get the best results, it's important to place your raised beds in the right spot in your outdoor space to provide the best conditions for the plants you decide to grow. Most cut flowers require a sunny area and fertile but free-draining soil. Raised beds can offer exactly that. You can improve the fertility of your soil in your raised bed by adding organic matter or growing green manure, which will help with soil structure.

Each raised bed is like a miniature garden. There are many ways of designing it, depending on the size of your space. Even the smallest cutting garden can give you buckets of gorgeous flowers. If planned carefully, a cutting garden in raised beds can also add a lot of interest to your outdoor space.

Many plants grown for cutting will add wonderful textures and colours, while annual grasses such as *Lagurus ovatus* or *Hordeum jubatum* will add movement and can look magical in the evening sun. Placing a bench or a few chairs next to your raised bed and watching your flowers grow will feel like a double happiness.

The perfect pick

When choosing plants to grow for cut flowers, think of those that will offer you a long season of picking – and there are so many! You can extend the cutting season by planting in spring and autumn. Think of your favourite colours and choose the plants that will create a lovely combination and result in the bouquets of your dreams.

When you start planting and sowing, please consider the final spread of plants. This information is easily accessible on seed packets or online. If you plant in rows (the most efficient way), don't make them too close together; I usually leave 30–45cm (12–18in) between the rows. You'll need to have enough space to access and harvest your flowers and do some weeding.

PLANT LIST

All the plants suggested here are easy to grow and suitable for complete beginners, giving peace of mind that they're going to perform. Many also have a dual purpose as both fresh and dry flowers (statice, celosia, strawflowers, foxtail barley, and nigella's dry seed heads).

Salvia / *Salvia viridis* 'Oxford Blue'
Statice / *Limonium sinuatum* 'Purple Attraction'
Cerinthe / *Cerinthe major* 'Purpurascens'
Celosia / *Celosia argentea* var. *spicata* 'True Wild Form'
Strawflower / *Acroclinium* 'Double Giant Flowered Mixed'
Foxtail barley / *Hordeum jubatum*
Nigella / *Nigella damascena* 'Miss Jekyll White'
Cosmos / *Cosmos bipinnatus* 'Gazebo White'

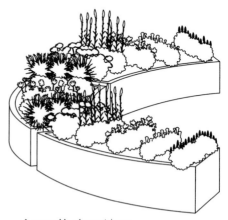

A curved bed provides a stunning panorama of flowers to admire from an enclosed seating area or to cut for display.

The white selection of nigella provides a pale foil to more colourful flowers in displays.

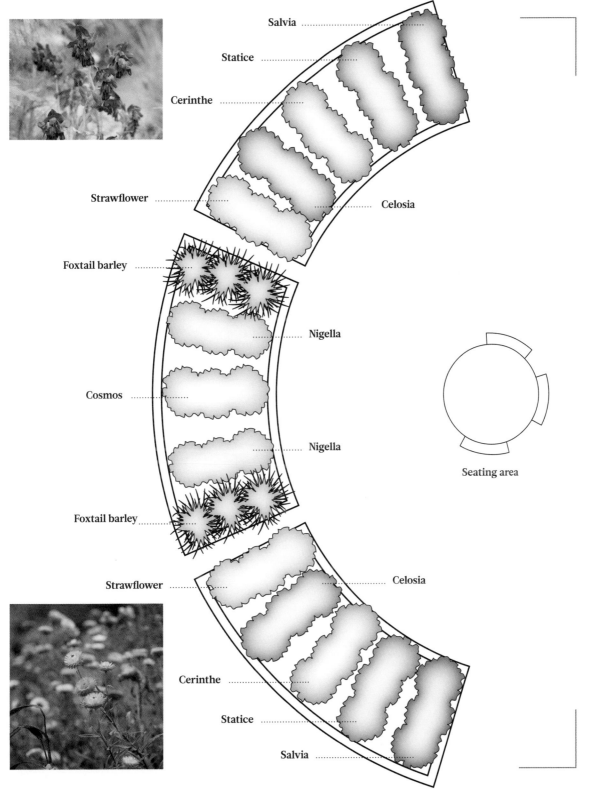

Salvia

Statice

Cerinthe

Strawflower

Celosia

Foxtail barley

Nigella

Cosmos

Nigella

Foxtail barley

Strawflower

Celosia

Cerinthe

Statice

Salvia

Seating area

Water-loving plants and pond life

There's no doubt that ponds are invaluable for wildlife, but they also create strong visual features and help to moderate temperatures in your plot. Meanwhile, bog gardens can teem with life, too, so why not bring them up closer to eye level where you can get in on the action?

Raise your game

A pool of water will bring so many benefits to your growing space, whatever its size. In small gardens and courtyards, as well as on balconies, however, digging down to set a pond into the ground may be impractical or laborious.

A raised pond could be the ideal solution, while also lifting the water surface up to reveal all the natural beauty it contains. And if the supporting wall is made wide enough, it can create an edge to sit on to gaze into the shadowy depths, at the same time as helping to insulate the water from cold penetrating in through the sides in winter.

A raised pool comes with safety benefits, too, making it less likely for children and animals to accidentally fall in. And while the elevated surface and sides may not be easily accessible to all types of garden wildlife, setting the pond into a bank or against another raised bed of soil should overcome this if required.

The benefits of water

Incorporate a waterfall spout or fountain into the raised pond and the sound will be captivating, as well as helping to mask road and other unwanted noise. Perhaps the least-known benefits, however, come from the properties of water itself. Not only will moisture evaporate from the surface to increase humidity for surrounding plants, but also water moderates temperature. This is due to its high specific heat capacity – meaning that it is slow to heat up and cool down – and the bigger the surface area of the pond, the more this comes into play.

Tiered raised ponds create sound and movement with falling water.

Choose plants with
a range of different
planting depths to make
best use of a raised pond.

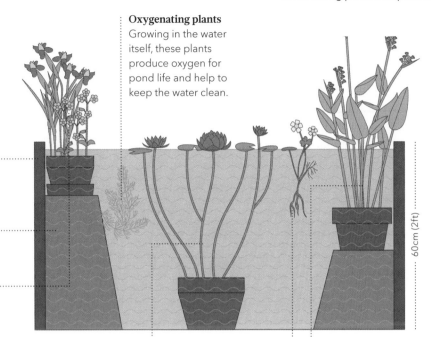

Oxygenating plants
Growing in the water
itself, these plants
produce oxygen for
pond life and help to
keep the water clean.

Liner Retain water in the
pond using a PVC or butyl
liner, or make the pond
with a pre-formed tank.

Marginal shelves Build
inside the pond to lift
marginal plants.

Shallow marginal plants
With their roots and
the base of the stems
covered in water up
to 15cm (6in) deep,
planted in baskets of
aquatic compost.

60cm (2ft)

Waterlilies Rooted in
baskets of aquatic
compost at the base of
the pond, with floating
leaves and flowers.

Free-floating plants
Growing just below the
surface, the foliage and
flowers of these plants
emerge above the water.

**Deep-water marginal
plants** Grow in baskets
of aquatic compost
around the edges of
the pond in water up
to 30cm (12in) deep.

Plants for raised ponds

There are plenty of beautiful
aquatic plants that will look
good and transform a raised
pond into a haven for wildlife.

Shallow marginal plants: Bog arum
(*Calla palustris*), flowering rush
(*Butomus umbellatus*), and water iris
(*Iris laevigata*), to name but a few.

Waterlilies: Choose varieties to suit
the depth of your pond – for example,
Nymphaea 'Pygmaea Helvola' in
water up to 30cm (12in) deep,
N. 'Froebelii' for 40cm (16in), and
N. 'Gonnère' for 50–60cm (20–24in).

Submerged plants: A range of types
includes willow moss (*Fontinalis
antipyretica*), water violet (*Hottonia
palustris*), and common water
crowfoot (*Ranunculus aquatilis*).

Deep-water marginal plants:
Choices include bogbean
(*Menyanthes trifoliata*), lesser
spearwort (*Ranunculus flammula*),
and powdery alligator-flag
(*Thalia dealbata*).

Waterlilies are the crowning
glory of the aquatic plant world.

Heat is absorbed from the surrounding atmosphere during the day and in hot weather, while being retained at night and during the cold months of the year. Thus, you and your plants will be able to enjoy a more even microclimate in your plot.

Welcoming pond life

A pond can also be brought to life by planting and by adding fish, or simply by leaving nature to take its course. In the latter case, you'll find that a host of aquatic animals appear in the water within a matter of weeks. These, in turn, will provide food for amphibians such as frogs, toads, and newts, as well as birds, reptiles, and mammals. Plus, the pond will instantly become a valuable source of water for wildlife.

Japanese primrose (*Primula japonica*) is one of many plants that suit a bog garden.

Iris ensata

Primula japonica

Matteuccia struthiopteris

Rheum palmatum

Astilbe

45–60cm (1½–2ft)

A raised bog garden could be used in conjunction with the pond, or perhaps as an alternative to it. Lined with polythene and filled with a mix of good-quality soil and well-rotted organic matter, this will create a root environment that retains plenty of water and nutrients for the lush, leafy growth of moisture-loving plants.

Waterproof liner to retain moisture in the bed.

Organic matter and top soil planting mix.

Landscape fabric membrane to stop soil washing into drainage layer.

Bog-garden plants: These need constant supplies of moisture from the soil and benefit from having around 8–10cm (3–4in) of soil above the permanent saturation level. Includes ornamental rhubarb (*Rheum palmatum*), Japanese primrose (*Primula japonica*), and European globeflower (*Trollius europaeus*), but there are many more.
NB: Check that any water, marginal, and bog plants are not considered invasive species in your area.

Spiked holes in sides for excess water to drain off.

Gravel drainage layer to act as a moisture reservoir.

Tailor growing to the climate

Keen gardeners will always try to push the limits of what they can grow in their climate. But whether it's succulents, bananas, or pineapples, raised beds can help meet their needs.

Temperate climates provide great conditions for growing a wide range of ornamental plants from around the world and have shaped the way we garden in Britain, Ireland, and much of Western Europe. Likewise, our taste in plants has been emulated around the globe, not only in places with similar weather conditions, but in both hotter and colder climates, too. Such aspirations have always led to struggles, not least with light levels, seasonality, soil types, altitude, rainfall, and, of course, temperature. And attempts to overcome these and grow something unusual, against all the odds, have allowed us to develop special techniques and refine the art of gardening. The taste for growing "exotic" plants in a temperate climate, for example, requires adding plenty of drainage material to the soil (in the form of grit or perlite) and providing shelter from cold weather.

Adaptation leads to invention

The more dramatic and unusual the plant, the more effort tends to go into the growing of it. Roses and delphiniums are seen as the archetypal English flowers, and many gardeners wish to grow them in unsuitable locations – in near-desert conditions in California and Australia, for example, where heat and light are intense, winter cold is almost unheard of, and soils are much less well developed than in the UK or other temperate regions.

Once again, raised beds offer a way to manipulate the growing environment. Both roses and delphiniums enjoy being able to root deeply into dense soil that is both cool and moist, so large, deep beds filled with a mix of heavy clay soil and plenty of well-rotted organic matter will go some way to satisfy their requirements in hot, dry regions.

Such a depth of soil to root into is also useful to help insulate the roots of plants from intense cold. The mix used to fill raised beds in this instance needs to be open-structured and free-draining to prevent waterlogging during prolonged periods of heavy rainfall. In continental Europe, Asia, and North America, large, deep beds can be used to protect root and tuber crops, as well as ornamental plants such as oriental poppies and peonies from sitting in cold, wet soil that could easily freeze in winter.

Undoubtedly such cultural manipulation has extended our knowledge in growing. The techniques involved will continue to be adapted and refined to cope with future challenges, but there is also a sense that gardening has come of age in so many countries: gardeners are using plants more suited to local conditions and valuing indigenous plants both in the wild and in cultivation. This is increasingly important amid a host of environmental concerns.

Tailor raised beds to suit specific plants like deep-rooting, moisture-loving delphiniums.

Lift up the lawn

A green sward is often seen as an essential design element in a garden, providing a unifying foil for all the other colours in beds and borders. But the lawn is also a place to sit out and entertain, so try raising it to extend its seasons of use.

Hard-wearing turf

Often we put lawns centre stage in our gardens, where they get the most use and are most visible. However, particularly on heavy soil, the worn surface can become compacted and muddy, causing the grass to weaken and other invasive species to get a foothold, affecting the quality of the lawn.

A raised-bed lawn offers a great solution. It can be filled with a gritty soil mixed with plenty of organic matter, then sown or turfed with good-quality grass, which will look good and take lots of use. It also means that the surface will dry out quickly after rain, and it will help to encourage deep rooting of the grass plants, making them more able to cope with dry weather. The edges of the raised lawn are easy to trim and will hold their form rather than collapsing into the surrounding borders.

Raising the lawn means that it can shed moisture more rapidly, preventing disease and helping to keep the grass healthy.

A lawn for lounging

In small or medium-sized plots, you could use this method to transform the whole lawn area. Where this isn't practical or affordable, a smaller "lounging" lawn could be created in a sunny spot by building a 20–30cm (8–12in) high raised bed containing the free-draining soil mixture. In the meantime, on a smaller scale, you could use a 50cm (20in) tall bed as the basis for a raised turf-topped seat. But whatever type of lawn you create, remember that it will be tougher and harder wearing if you leave it 3–7cm (1¼–2¾in) long, rather than cutting it too short, which will stress the grass plants.

Small raised beds can be used to create mini lawns to use as seating areas.

Requiring less maintenance that a standard lawn but able to take only limited use, these grass alternatives are ideal to top a raised bed or create a green roof.

Thyme
For summer flowers and evergreen, aromatic foliage, creeping thymes offer an easy-care alternative to grass in a raised bed. The plants are surprisingly tough, and will take occasional use for lounging on. Create a tapestry with swirls of different foliage and flower colour forms. Best in full sun.

Chamomile
Make sure you use lawn chamomile (*Chamaemelum nobile* 'Treneague') for a close-growing, neat effect. Strongly fragrant foliage will release its scent when walked or lain on. Can cope with light use in dry weather. Clip lightly after flowering to keep plants neat. Does well in sun or part shade.

Sedum
The mat-forming species of this succulent genus are well adapted to heat, drought, and cold if grown in free-draining soil. Different foliage colours and flowers can be used to weave attractive patterns for a raised lawn. Easy to grow from small pieces that break off. Best in full sun or part shade.

Curating a collection

The wonderful detail in the structure of plants is often best seen close up, especially for the more diminutive types, such as alpines. Meanwhile, rare and difficult-to-cultivate species can be catered and cared for by creating bespoke growing conditions in raised beds.

Plants on a pedestal

So many of us have favourite plants that we love to grow and collect in some way. This can be in the form of different species, varieties, and flower colours of the same genus, or a particular type of plant, such as ferns or conifers.

While these plants can be spread around in various parts of the garden, planting them together in a raised bed helps to celebrate their diversity and allows them to be compared. And, like any group of plants, they usually share similar soil requirements and growing conditions, which means that these can be tailored specifically to their needs when grouped together.

The curator's choice

Choosing what to grow will obviously be down to individual taste, but it is worth considering the plants' seasons of interest. Different species may bloom at different times, which will extend the display, as with the *Primula* genus, for example, which has winter-, spring-, and early-summer-flowering species. Meanwhile, leaf shape, form, and colour, as well as seedheads and fruit, can all be taken into account so there's something to draw the eye for as long as possible. Another option is to combine two plant groups with different seasons of display: summer-flowering geraniums interplanted with small-growing spring bulbs, for example, will help get the most out of the raised bed.

Many gardeners like to grow plants from a particular genus as a demonstration for themselves, or to conserve diversity of varieties that might otherwise disappear. This is made all the more crucial if plants are endangered or extinct in their native environment. The UK is fortunate to have many National Collections, which are maintained by large private gardens, state-owned institutions, botanical gardens, and educational establishments, as well as by individuals in their back gardens.

Filled with a gritty growing medium, this sunny raised bed is ideal for a collection of bearded iris.

Plants for a special collection

These popular groups of plants make ideal candidates for growing as a mixture of different species and varieties. Extend the season of interest by underplanting them with various spring-flowering bulbs.

Acers
Grown for form and colour. Choose a sheltered location, away from drying wind and full sun at midday. Use a free-draining soil mix with plenty of well-rotted leaf mould.

Dwarf conifers
Grown for overall form, winter colour, and cones. Choose an open, well-lit site with space to allow them to develop good shape. Use an open, well-drained, acid-to-neutral soil.

Epimediums
Grown for spring flowers, foliage, and autumn colour. Prefers shade or part shade. They like moisture-retentive, acid-to-neutral soil with plenty of organic matter.

Ferns
Grown for form, foliage shape and colour. Grow in partial or dappled shade, avoiding full sun. Add organic matter to the soil mix to maintain moisture levels without waterlogging.

Geraniums
Grown for summer flowers, foliage, and ground cover. Grow in full sun or part shade. Use an open, well-drained soil mix, neutral to alkaline, with well-rotted organic matter.

Hellebores
Grown for late-winter to spring flowers and year-round foliage. Grow in part shade – avoid full sun. Use well-drained soil, with plenty of organic matter to retain moisture in summer.

Heucheras
Grown for colourful, year-round foliage and summer flowers. Prefer part or dappled shade and moisture-retentive soil, with good drainage. Add well-rotted organic matter.

Iris
Grown for flower form and colour. Prefers an open site in full sun. Use a well-drained soil mix with organic matter. Most benefit from a neutral-to-alkaline soil.

Ornamental grasses
Grown for form, colour, flowers, and seedheads. Choose an open site with plenty of sun to allow typical form to develop. Use gritty, free-draining soil with some organic matter.

Catering for a special diet

Some species of plants nourish themselves in unconventional ways, and carnivorous plants are a prime example. Understanding the natural environment in which these curious plants originate will help with their cultivation at home, and a raised bed is the perfect place to do this.

This lined raised bed holds plentiful moisture for these frost-hardy sarracenias.

Food for carnivores

While the majority of plants gain the nutrients they need from the soil, carnivorous species have evolved in challenging habitats where certain chemicals are lacking. These intriguing plants have developed mechanisms to gather many crucial nutrients by capturing insects. They do this with fascinating leaf adaptations, including, among others, having water-fill pitcher traps (pitcher plants), sticky leaves (sundews), or even toothed trigger traps (Venus flytrap).

The terrestrial species of carnivorous plants grow in acidic peat bogs in the wild, where poor drainage leads to a saturated soil environment at certain times of the year. A raised bed lined with polythene or butyl will retain moisture, in the same way as if creating a bog garden. However, the soil mix in this case would need to be lime-free and very low in nutrients and, ideally, amid growing environmental concerns, peat-free.

Peat-free growing

Sustainably produced sphagnum moss, which some types of peat are ultimately formed from, has been trialled by growers and societies, and has proved suitable. Meanwhile, coir chunks, which are a by-product from coconut husks, are recommended as an alternative for peat by some growers and societies, although the material needs to be lime-free and not washed in seawater. However, remember that the coconut-growing industry has its own environmental issues to address.

Ultimately a raised bed with a liner, which can always be kept moist, has the major advantage for growing carnivorous plants, in dramatically slowing decomposition of the growing medium – whether coir, sphagnum, or peat – compared to pot cultivation. And the humid environment that is created will be better for the plants.

There is a wide range of carnivorous plants that grow in the ground, making them suitable for large planters or raised beds.

Hardy species that can be grown outside in cool climates or in an unheated greenhouse. A collection could include:

California pitcher plant (*Darlingtonia californica*)

Sundew (*Drosera filiformis, D. × hybrida, D. rotundifolia*)

Large-flowered butterwort (*Pinguicula grandiflora*)

Pitcher plant (*Sarracenia alata, S. flava, S. oreophila, S. purpurea*, and many hybrids)

Tender species that can be grown outdoors in moist and frost-free regions, or indoors in cool or cold climates. A collection could include:

Powdery strap airplant (*Catopsis berteroniana, C. morreniana,* and *C. floribunda*)

Australian pitcher plant (*Cephalotus follicularis*)

Venus flytrap (*Dionaea muscipula*)

Cape and spoon-leaved sundew (*Drosera capensis* and *D. spatulata*)

Marsh pitcher plant (*Heliamphora pulchella, H. heterodoxa,* and *H. nutans*)

Butterwort (*Pinguicula agnata, P. esseriana, P. gigantea,* and *P. vulgaris*)

Bladderwort (*Utricularia gibba, U. sandersonii,* and *U. vulgaris*)

Clockwise from top:
Sarracenia hybrid; *S. oreophila; Catopsis berteroniana; Utricularia sandersonii; Drosera filiformis.*

Designing for drought

Faced with a changing climate, gardeners need to adapt to suit the new normal. And as water becomes an ever more precious resource, drought-resistant planting is gaining in popularity.

The challenge of extreme weather

We all want a moisture-retentive yet free-draining soil, but the reality for many is either heavy and wet, or free-draining and dry. In extreme weather, this means either too much water or not enough.

To cope with excess heat and a lack of rain in summer, drought-tolerant plants provide a very real solution, but they can't shrug off excess water, particularly in the dormant season. For them to survive, it's crucial that the soil is adapted for them, and with shallow raised beds, filled with an open-structured soil and organic-matter mix, you can effectively create an ideal topsoil.

Once established, drought-tolerant species will need little or no additional watering due to a range of useful adaptations to conserve moisture in the plant tissues, some of which add to their charm.

Clever adaptations

Most attractive are the foliage adaptations, such as grey or silver coloration to reflect the heat of the sun, and hairy leaves that trap humidity around the surface of the plant to reduce evaporation. Other modifications include waxy coatings, resinous concentrated sap, and needle-like foliage, which drastically reduces its surface area for water loss.

Succulents and cacti are well adapted to water conservation, too, with few, if any, leaves. Their stems are filled with cells that can take on the job of making sugars as well as store water. They also have thick, waxy surfaces to reduce evaporation.

Meanwhile, many drought-resistant species are able to root deeply. This allows them to tap into water further down in the soil and store moisture to prevent the plants drying out in times of low rainfall.

Lining metal troughs with insulating layers of recycled carpet reduces the amount of heat penetrating through the sides.

Top drought-tolerant plants

These plants show good drought tolerance and contain species that are hardy to at least -10°C (14°F). Combine in a bed filled with sharply drained soil and organic matter for a tough display that looks good into the future.

Artemisia
Woody perennial, with finely filigreed silver-grey foliage, which is strongly aromatic. Spikes of white flowers in the summer.

Echinops
Fleshy rooted herbaceous perennial, which grows from a basal clump of grey-green foliage. Stems are topped with golf-ball globes of flowers.

Eryngium
Silver-green holly-like foliage, which grows from a basal clump of semi-evergreen foliage. Intense blue flower clusters in summer.

Euphorbia
Wide range of herbaceous perennial forms, which are topped with chrome yellow bracts surrounding tiny flowers in late spring or early summer.

Halimium
Compact woody perennial with fine twigs and grey-green foliage. Bears plentiful flowers in late spring and early summer.

Juniper
Bushy conifer, which comes in a range of different forms. Woody stems are covered with fine, pointed needles. Berries in autumn.

Lavender
Woody shrubs with fine blue-green, needle-like foliage, which is highly aromatic. Flower spikes carried in early to late summer.

Santolina
Compact, woody bush with delicate leaves that are strongly aromatic. Balls of yellow flowers are produced in summer.

Verbascum
Rosette-forming, herbaceous perennials or biennials with tall flower spikes carrying lots of flowers from early to late summer.

Tropical foliage plants require protection from frost in temperate climates.

Homes for houseplants

Raised beds don't need to be the preserve of outdoor spaces. Indoor planters allow block planting of a single species or a mixture of plants to be grown together. This takes houseplant growing to another level, providing a better rooting environment with a steady supply of moisture and nutrients.

In temperate climates like those in much of Europe and North America, protected growing is necessary for the huge range of plants that originate in the subtropics and tropics – in particular from the floor of the rainforests. They benefit from even, moderate temperatures and high humidity. Perhaps surprisingly, many of them are adapted to low light levels, so positioning a large planter or built-in raised bed in a well-lit room, close to a window, where the lower temperate light levels are broadly equivalent to those on the forest floor, should provide ideal conditions.

In summer, most houseplant species can be moved outdoors to a sheltered, part-shaded position – as long as night-time temperatures don't dip below around 10°C (50°F). In addition, there are lots of tender flowering species – often from Mediterranean-style climates, such as oleander, bougainvillea, and plumbago – which can go outdoors in summer but should be moved into a glasshouse, conservatory, or the home for winter. Or they can be grown permanently in a well-lit conservatory.

Succulent species from hot, low-rainfall regions make great houseplants, too. Many of these have deep roots, which help them survive drought, so an indoor raised bed filled with gritty, free-draining soil will suit them well, rather than restrict them as in small pots.

Large planters or raised beds also offer a great way to grow tender plants and seasonal crops in glasshouses and polythene tunnels, especially where these are constructed on a paved surface with no open soil in which to plant. This will extend the growing season in temperate parts of the world.

Protected growing for exotic plants

The home environment offers a great opportunity to extend the range of species that gardeners can grow. By offering protected environments both outdoors and in, there is a whole world of plant possibilities to choose from.

Stylish mixed plantings can be grown in indoor raised beds, as in this heated conservatory.

Temperate plants in hot climates

By contrast, in hotter climates, protected growing can shield vulnerable plants from the excess heat and desiccating effects of the sun. Here, shelter can take the form of an unglazed shade house, covered either with close-woven shade netting or timber lathes. This also traps humidity inside to the plants' benefit, as well as giving protection from heavy rain and hail. Using deep raised beds filled with a moisture-retentive soil mix, you can then grow shade-loving and delicate-leaved species.

And in hot, dry climates, this kind of set-up also suits the cultivation of tropical rainforest plants.

With growing conditions becoming more extreme in the face of climate change, such a combination of shade and soil management will become increasingly necessary in order to grow vulnerable plants in future, as well as expanding the range of plants we can cultivate.

Raising new plants

There is a great sense of achievement in growing your own new plants, and a raised bed for propagation will earn its keep by saving you money. Plus, it'll help you hone your horticultural skills and enjoy the benefits of "slow" gardening.

Setting up a propagation bed

Planting up a new garden or adding seasonal plants to your plot is a costly business if everything is sourced as pot-grown stock from garden centres and nurseries. Growing your own from seed or cuttings will cut those costs dramatically, and while it might take time and patience, it is easy to propagate a very wide range of plants.

Setting up your own propagation area is relatively straightforward. A propagator indoors is a useful addition for cold-season sowing and for softwood cuttings, but it's not essential. A small raised bed in a glasshouse, polythene tunnel,

sheltered corner outdoors, or on a balcony can be filled with gritty compost and used to raise seeds and cuttings during the warm season.

Retaining warmth and moisture will speed up the process of germination or rooting, and there are a few options that can be used. Incorporating a glazed, removable lid is ideal and has been used for hundreds of years as the basis for the outdoor cold frame. But you could also use individual cloches over seed rows or batches of cuttings and, on a smaller scale, glass jars or cut-down plastic drinks bottles.

Where the bed is made under cover, additional warmth can be provided with electric heating mats or cables under the compost. This is particularly useful when raising annual seeds and cuttings early in the growing season, but it's not essential, and certainly not necessary in the warmest months.

However, for hardy seeds and sowing in the warmest months, such covering is unnecessary as long as the seedlings are kept regularly watered. And in the winter months (in temperate climates), seeds of hardy trees, shrubs, and perennials will benefit from exposure to the cold in order to break any seed dormancy. Meanwhile, hardwood cuttings will survive uncovered, too.

The propagation bed itself can be shallow; as little as 10cm (4in) will provide adequate depth for rooting into. It pays to make it a little deeper – around 20cm (8in) – for rooting larger types of cuttings. Fill the bed with a gritty compost mix and refresh each season to help reduce diseases that could cause your seeds and cuttings to fail.

What to grow in a nursery bed

The seeds of some vegetables can be sown in a propagation or "nursery" bed to bring them on to a size ready to plant out in their final growing positions. This will help save space and optimize productivity by having new plants ready to go in once previous crops have been harvested.

A raised "nursery" bed with an insulating and protective cover is great for rooting cuttings or raising plants from seed.

This technique is also suitable for hardy and half-hardy annual flowers, biennials, and herbaceous perennials grown from seed. In addition, you can grow hardy shrubs and trees from autumn-sown seed, to germinate in the following spring and summer.

When it comes to raising plants from cuttings, such a bed is most suitable for slow-to-root stem cuttings (see panel below), while root cuttings can also be taken from plants in the dormant season.

While not everything can be raised from seed and cuttings in the domestic environment, there are many plants that can – and many rewards to be had.

Semi-ripe cuttings taken in summer are easy to root in a covered cold-frame bed.

Cuttings for a cold frame

A cold-frame bed includes a glass or Perspex lid, which can be used to protect the cuttings from the cold, as well as allowing warmth to build up to speed rooting, while maintaining humidity to prevent wilting leaves. Softwood cuttings are best rooted in pots or trays in a propagator but can be planted out in a cold frame, once rooted, to grow on. The following cuttings can be rooted directly into the soil and compost mix in a cold-frame bed:

Greenwood (pliable stems that are still green in colour)
When to take:
Late spring and summer
What to take: Hardy and tender plants such as: argyranthemum, buddleia, ceanothus, chrysanthemums, fuchsia (pictured), hebe, hydrangea, lavatera, lonicera, osteospermum, pelargonium, penstemon, roses, verbena.

Semi-ripe (firm stems that are changing colour from green to russet or brown)
When to take:
Mid- to late summer
What to take: Shrubs such as: artemisia, berberis, brachyglottis, camellia, ceanothus, choisya, cistus, escallonia, hyssop, ilex, laurus, lavender (pictured), ligustrum, rosemary, salvia, solanum, trachelospermum and viburnum.

Hardwood (woody stems of the current season's growth)
When to take:
Autumn and late winter
What to take: Shrubs such as: cornus, deutzia (pictured), forsythia, ribes, roses, sambucus, philadelphus, and salix. Fruiting plants such as: blackberries, currants, figs, gooseberries, mulberries, and grapevines.

Designing a bed

Design approaches

So far in this book, we've looked at the pros and cons of raised beds and seen some of the inspiring ways in which they can be used to grow plants. When it comes to designing them for your own plot, it's worth going through a carefully considered process so that you end up with something that will be useful, practical, attractive, and on budget.

Form and function

At their simplest, raised beds can take the form of shallow retaining timber edges, topped up with good-quality soil and compost to form an ideal topsoil in which to plant. But more elaborate

Raised beds can be used to lift plants and provide more vertical scale in the garden.

Tall beds can be positioned at the centre of a plot to make a feature where they will get optimum light.

Bold, chunky beds suit this simple, modern garden design.

designs, with multiple structures built from brick, blockwork, or stone, could form the backbone of any garden, courtyard, balcony, or rooftop plot.

As with any aspect of garden design, there are some basics to follow on form and function. The most successful raised beds should not only offer practical solutions for growing, but look good, too: after all, you'll have to spend a significant proportion of your time looking at them as well as gardening in them - especially if they can be seen from indoors.

While it might come as a bit of a surprise, from the outset one of the most important design considerations is whether you actually need raised beds or not. There are plenty of inspirational gardens that don't use them at all and many others with raised beds that look jumbled and overdesigned. Ultimately, you should use these structures for a reason, rather than just for the sake of it, particularly given the effort and potential cost involved in making them. Take time to think if they will help you garden better, perform a useful function, or add to the look of your plot.

Shallow walls make defined edges to contain soil and keep paths clean.

Complex sloping sites can incorporate steps with raised beds to accommodate changes in level.

In small spaces keep designs simple, using a few geometric shapes - squares, rectangles, and circles - to avoid making the space appear too fussy and cluttered.

Integrated design

Having rationalized your thoughts on why you want raised beds, it's important to consider how they might fit into your plot. Mostly, this will be a matter of personal preference and taste, but it is worth thinking about the context of your home and growing space, and how they interact.

The most successful garden designs take inspiration from their accompanying building, with the hard landscaping – retaining walls, paving, structures, and seating – reflecting its style and the materials it is built from. This may inform the design, shape, and size of any raised beds you install. An integrated, ground-up approach is likely to produce a harmonious result and is most appropriate for new-build or renovation projects. In pre-established plots, however, adding raised beds needs careful consideration. Building them from recycled pallet timber, for example, can look out of place in a modern plot and slick stainless-steel planters might look incongruous in a cottage garden.

Urban, suburban, and rural inspiration

As well as being guided by your building, you could take your design cues from the surrounding environment, to better reflect and blend in with your landscape.

If you live in a rural location where stone is mostly used for building, it pays to choose the prevailing local material for making your raised beds, or at least something that has a similar look and texture. The buildings in urban and suburban areas are likely to be built from a range of materials, many of them manufactured, with bricks, tiles, and metal

Contrasting materials and colours are a great way to introduce interest (left); natural walls and plantings help soften the stark lines of modern architecture (right).

Raised beds can make eye-catching features near the house, while the walls can incorporate garden lighting (left); white rendered walls help reflect light into dark spaces (right).

predominating. Taking care to use sympathetic materials will bring cohesion to a successful design, which will make it great to look at and more satisfying to live with.

For unity, an individual raised bed is best built out of a single material, rather than cobbling it together from a mishmash of all sorts. In many cases it can also be appropriate to construct multiple beds out of the same material to create a unified look. Such uniformity would be complementary to the design of a medium-to-large formal garden, taking its inspiration from the grand gardens of country houses and estates. But using the same material for a number of different shapes and sizes of raised bed can also create visual coherence in a small city courtyard or on a balcony.

Material matters

For a more eclectic and less formal look, it is possible to make individual beds out of different materials to provide visual contrasts. However, it is important to think about their surface textures and different colours from the outset. Shiny stainless-steel often appears awkward beside red brick, and rough-surfaced orange "Carstone" makes an odd bedfellow for smooth black slate. More suitable combinations might include a mix of planed timber and COR-TEN (rusting) steel, rough natural stone and smooth brick, or stainless-steel and slate. And as with most aspects of design, it's worth applying the mantra "less is more" in this instance: too many different materials will look jumbled and messy.

The way in which light reflects off surfaces is another key consideration, particularly in small spaces where they will be most noticeable. Dark, matte textures will blend in and become recessive, while pale, reflective materials tend to stand out and dominate. Polished metal and highly glazed tile finishes are particularly reflective and often suggested for bouncing light into dark corners, but they can also create dazzle and glare when the sun is low in the sky.

Siting raised beds

Before we get on with looking in detail at the different construction materials and some variations in the form that raised beds can take, it is worth looking at a range of other considerations that may inform your decisions. Most important of these is their situation.

Where such beds form part of an overall design, their position may be governed by the size, shape, and layout of the growing space, and as a result plants will need to be chosen to suit the growing conditions in that location, rather than selecting the ideal situation. Depending on the orientation of buildings and other structures, as well as other plantings, this could mean a position in full sun, in varying degrees of shade, exposed to wind, or in a rain shadow (the latter resulting in dry conditions).

This scenario is most common in very small gardens, courtyards, and balconies, as well as in the area immediately to the back or front of a building. Such constraint may mean that planting varies between different beds in individual parts of the plot. Alternatively, the number of species used could be limited to things that are able to thrive in such varied conditions.

While it is best to position raised beds on top of existing soil (however poor it might be – see Chapter 4, page 190), they can also be installed over solid surfaces. Cast concrete, paving slabs, tarmac, compacted hardcore, gravel, and roofing materials can provide a base on which to build.

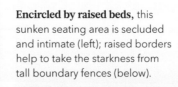

Encircled by raised beds, this sunken seating area is secluded and intimate (left); raised borders help to take the starkness from tall boundary fences (below).

Choosing a place to grow

In temperate climates, the optimum growing position for many plants is one that receives good light levels, where they can get natural rainfall and are sheltered from the worst wind. A nearby water source may also be an advantage.

Potential frost pocket in winter: Boundary fences and walls create shade from morning sun and trap cold air at their base.

Frost pocket and wind exposure: This area can remain cold and frosty for much of the day, until the sun moves round to warm it.

Water butt

Rain shadows from house: Tall walls and eaves can prevent rain getting to beds sited in their lee.

Sheltered from wind: A protected spot in full sun is the ideal site for most raised beds.

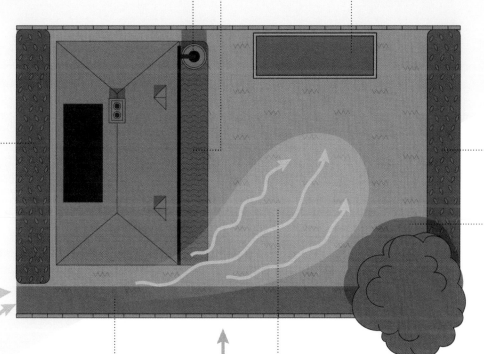

Prevailing wind: The strongest and most frequent winds will leave plants vulnerable to physical damage and drying out.

Sun at midday

Area exposed to wind: Buildings and other structures can funnel wind to increase its damage potential.

Boundary shade: This can cause plants to become tall and leggy, and lean away from the boundary structure.

Tree shade: Large trees with dense canopies will cut out lots of light and stop rain getting to plants underneath.

A simple, slabbed path allows ready wheeled access to these vegetable beds.

Open positions are ideal for creating good air circulation and maximizing light levels for growth.

This can free up the potential for growing on sites that tick lots of the other suitability boxes. Make sure that the beds are deep enough for the plants that you wish to grow and ensure that there is ample drainage to prevent them becoming waterlogged.

Low raised beds can be used to subdivide a plot and thus create a more intimate feel.

The right conditions

If you wish to grow a specific range of plants, choose a situation for the raised beds that provides them with ideal conditions. In the case of productive cropping – vegetables, herbs, fruit, and cut flowers – an open position, with sun for at least half the day, would be preferable. This might be found away from boundary fences, walls, and buildings, in a medium-to-small plot or on some rooftop locations.

With plentiful light, the plants will be able to make lots of energy that will go into producing the best crop. Such open locations have the added

benefit of good air circulation, allowing the foliage of plants to dry out after rain – something that helps to limit the incidence of disease, which would otherwise spoil the harvest.

Sheltered environments

Some shelter from wind is useful, however, to protect the plants from the strongest gusts. A position downwind of a hedge or slatted fence

Here, a raised bed dissects the garden, helping to create distinct "rooms".

Where possible, it is best to site shallow raised beds away from such prone areas. However, taller beds will allow cold to drain off their surfaces.

Sites away from dense-crowned trees are preferable, too – not only because their roots suck water from the soil during the growing season; they also cast shade at particular times of day, causing the plants beneath to grow out on one side in search of light. The foliage of overhanging branches might prove problematic, too, preventing light rain getting through to the soil below or creating heavy, damaging drips during showers.

Meanwhile, infestations of aphids or other pests on the trees could exude sticky honeydew, which showers down onto the plants beneath, encouraging sooty, disfiguring mould on their leaves.

Growing in full sight

When considering where to position raised beds – particularly for crop growing – it's worth thinking about the availability of water nearby. As we've seen, free drainage is an intrinsic part of raising soil above the surrounding area, and keeping moisture at the plant roots during hot, dry weather will invariably involve regular watering. Ideally, collecting rainwater or grey water from buildings will supply these needs, and getting it onto the beds will be much easier if they are close by (see Chapter 5, page 225).

Being able to check crops regularly is also beneficial, whether it is looking out for signs of drought or pest and disease attack. Having the beds close to home means that you're more likely to see when veg, fruit, and flowers are ready to harvest. And popping out to pick herbs for use in the kitchen is easy if the beds are close to the back door!

Most ornamental plants will be more self-sufficient than productive plants, with the possible exception of seasonal bedding. It's still good to have raised beds of precious and unusual plants in full sight where they can be looked after with careful attention. Making the most of raised beds for intensive growing means you can look after other parts of the garden in a more low-maintenance way, planting them with trees, shrubs, and easy-care perennials. These will then provide the backdrop for the raised beds.

is the best option as the wind will be slowed but air can still circulate. Solid walls or fences often increase the wind on their leeward side to cause plant-damaging turbulence. In temperate climates, shelter can also trap warmth on sunny spring days to encourage growth – but remember that it may also compound heat at the height of summer or in hot climate zones.

Avoid siting raised beds close to heat sources and air vents, too. Lifting plants into the firing line can easily make them vulnerable. Regularly used barbecues, fire pits, and boiler flues will scorch nearby leaves and stems, causing physical damage, while the dry air expelled by extractor fans, air-conditioning units, and air-source heat pumps can quickly desiccate foliage, causing it to wilt or shrivel.

Another consideration in colder regions is that of frost pockets. In winter, cold air descends from the sky and drains down slopes and into valleys until it meets any obstructions. Here it collects to intensify the effects of cold and frost to damage the soft top growth of plants and penetrate into the soil. The worst pockets occur in valley bottoms and on the upside of walls, solid fences, and even evergreen hedges that run across open, sloping ground.

Accessibility and ease of use

Accessibility is a key design consideration for any grower, but especially for those with mobility restrictions, those gardening from a wheelchair, and those of a short stature.

The areas closest to the house lend themselves to the incorporation of paved surfaces in the form of patios, terraces, or paths, which provide convenient, clean, and level access to raised beds. Slabs and other solid materials are appropriate around mortared stone, brick, and metal retaining walls, and have the added benefit of providing stable wheeled access.

Further away from buildings, and where beds are built from timber, dry stone, or other, less formal materials, good-quality paths can be made of well-firmed, all-in ballast topped with a thin layer of gravel. This will produce a load-bearing surface that will support wheels.

A low-cost alternative would be to use chipped bark laid directly onto firmed soil surrounding the beds. This will take a fair amount of foot traffic to limit compaction and absorb mud during periods of wet weather.

By contrast, grass access paths, although natural looking, are liable to excessive wear, quickly becoming weedy, slippery, and muddy. Cutting the grass between raised beds is also challenging.

A functional slabbed path creates easy access, while gravel side paths allow rainwater to soak into the ground beneath the raised beds.

Designed for accessibility

As we saw in Chapter 1 (see page 38), raising the growing height makes great sense for ease of work, particularly for older gardeners or those with mobility limitations. But remember that such ease of access can benefit gardeners of any age to help prevent injury and strain.

For standing adults, it is important to bring the height up considerably – usually to 90cm (35in) – to reduce stooping, thus preventing back problems and providing a finished working surface to lean on. The finished height can be tailored to the specific needs and standing height of the user, requiring much the same considerations as those for kitchen worktops indoors.

Raised beds are also beneficial for wheelchair and seated access. In such instances, raising the

Wall tops can be used to bring pots of plants up to a more convenient height for planting and maintenance.

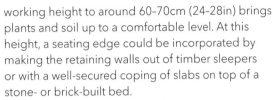

working height to around 60–70cm (24–28in) brings plants and soil up to a comfortable level. At this height, a seating edge could be incorporated by making the retaining walls out of timber sleepers or with a well-secured coping of slabs on top of a stone- or brick-built bed.

An equally important consideration is the finished width of the raised bed. Without too much uncomfortable stretching, it should be possible to access up to 60cm (24in) from one side of the bed in the standing position, at the working height suggested above. Where access can be gained from each side, this means that the finished bed width can be 1.2 metres (4ft), including the supporting walls. From a seated position or wheelchair, this width may be reduced to a maximum of 45cm (18in) from each side, unless long-handled tools are to be used.

For children, the working height and width will of course change as they get older. Toddlers may only be able to cope with beds around 45cm (18in) high and to stretch in 30cm (12in) from each side, while for older children beds can be taller and wider. A basic modular timber structure would cater for the growing needs of a young gardener, allowing one or two layers to be added progressively.

Incorporating seating into the edge of a raised bed provides somewhere to sit and rest.

Tall corner posts provide a convenient leaning point (left), and allow for added boards to raise the level of the bed if required (right).

An accessible veg patch

Emma Lovewell

When I was growing up my parents had an in-ground veg garden. Every year we would till the soil, adding in homemade compost, and try to tackle the weeds all summer long. In my own gardens, I've chosen to create multiple raised beds, initially because I was growing in urban areas with little room. Now that I have more land, I still choose raised beds.

Black kale is hardy, ornamental, delicious, and packed full of nutrients - an excellent addition to any vegetable bed.

Emma Lovewell is originally from Martha's Vineyard, Massachusetts. Her mother, Teresa Yuan, is a professional gardener on the island, designing flower containers and vegetable and flower gardens for many of her clients. Emma is a Peloton instructor, teaching fitness to millions globally, and has created a handful of gardens - even in cement courtyards in New York City.

She credits her mother with teaching her everything she knows about gardening. Emma now lives in the Hudson Valley with multiple gardens, her partner, Dave, and her two cats, Kimchi and Rhody.

www.livelearnlovewell.com
Instagram: @emmalovewell
TikTok: @emma_lovewell

We ordered our wooden beds online and put them together ourselves. Whether we plant from seed or seedling depends on the year. As I've got older and wiser, I've become braver about starting some plants from seed, such as lettuce, courgette, carrots, climbing beans, loofah, and cucumber. I've also discovered that herbs like basil and parsley are incredibly easy to grow from seed. That said, I know certain crops always turn out better when I buy seedlings from the garden nursery, and there's no shame in that: work smarter not harder!

One reason I prefer gardening with raised beds is that you can better control the soil medium. It's easier on your back, too, if the beds are high enough, as you don't have to bend down to ground level. Raised beds also make gardening more accessible, as they allow you to walk around them and reach all parts of the plot. You can prevent pests - in our case gophers - from digging under the beds, too, as long as you put some kind of landscaping cloth or wire underneath. On top of all that, I think raised garden beds look amazing and more organized.

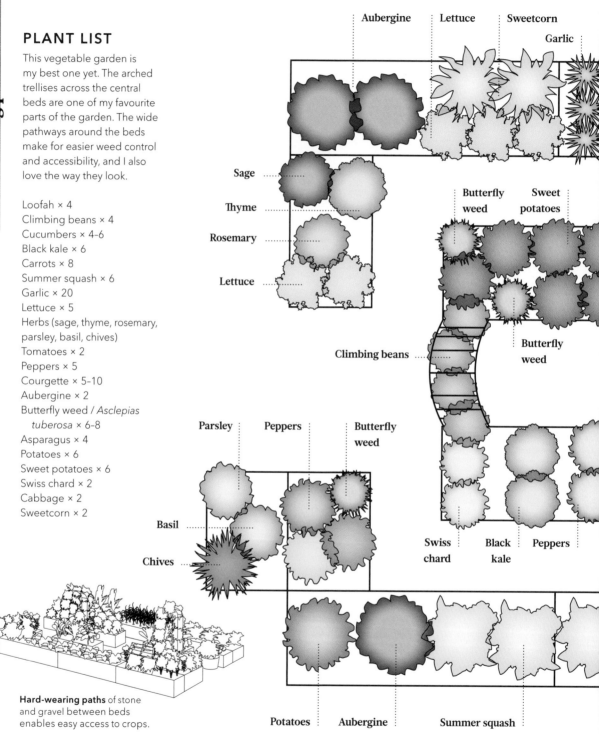

PLANT LIST

This vegetable garden is my best one yet. The arched trellises across the central beds are one of my favourite parts of the garden. The wide pathways around the beds make for easier weed control and accessibility, and I also love the way they look.

Loofah × 4
Climbing beans × 4
Cucumbers × 4-6
Black kale × 6
Carrots × 8
Summer squash × 6
Garlic × 20
Lettuce × 5
Herbs (sage, thyme, rosemary, parsley, basil, chives)
Tomatoes × 2
Peppers × 5
Courgette × 5-10
Aubergine × 2
Butterfly weed / *Asclepias tuberosa* × 6-8
Asparagus × 4
Potatoes × 6
Sweet potatoes × 6
Swiss chard × 2
Cabbage × 2
Sweetcorn × 2

Aubergine
Lettuce
Sweetcorn
Garlic

Sage
Thyme
Rosemary
Lettuce

Butterfly weed
Sweet potatoes

Climbing beans

Butterfly weed

Parsley
Peppers
Butterfly weed

Basil

Chives

Swiss chard
Black kale
Peppers

Potatoes
Aubergine
Summer squash

Hard-wearing paths of stone and gravel between beds enables easy access to crops.

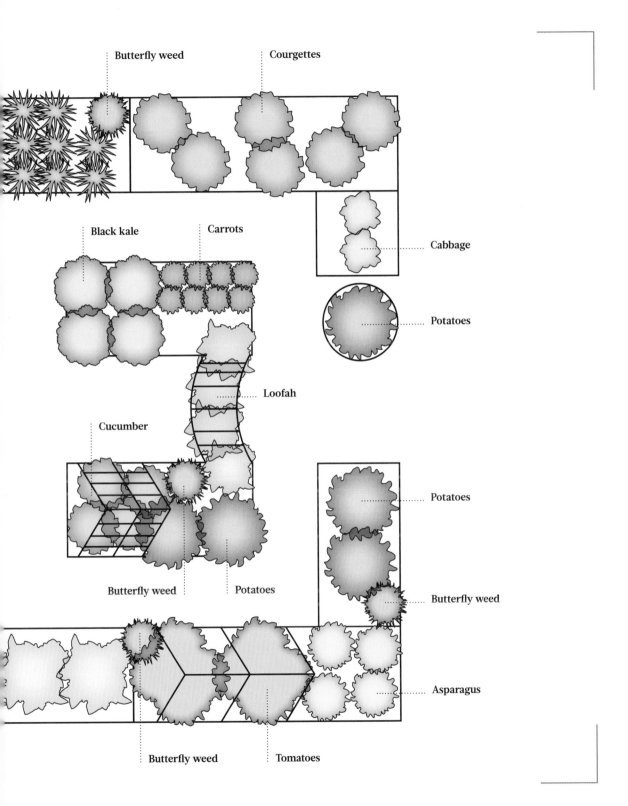

Butterfly weed

Courgettes

Cabbage

Black kale

Carrots

Potatoes

Loofah

Cucumber

Potatoes

Butterfly weed

Butterfly weed

Potatoes

Asparagus

Butterfly weed

Tomatoes

Raised bed shapes and forms

In plan, raised beds often take a rectangular or geometric shape – possibly because such forms are easy to draw and build. However, with an appropriate choice of building materials, they can take any form you want.

Their shape may be determined by the overall design of your garden – for example, a long, narrow raised border alongside a path or terrace. And generally, in a small garden, courtyard, or balcony, simple geometric shapes will fit in well: triangular borders are great for filling corners, while circular shapes make good centrepieces. Edging such beds with a shallow retaining wall of brick, or with timber sleepers, for example, would help to contain soil while also making maintenance easy.

In large plots, formally shaped geometric beds sit well close to the house and other garden buildings. Further away from such strong structural elements, borders can take on more curved and informal shapes, and this can follow through in the outlines of any raised beds.

An extra dimension

Your design can also take on three dimensions by using raised beds of different heights. A tall corner bed, for example, can be surrounded by intermediate-height beds to create a layered effect. Such structure will give visual interest and draw the eye, even in its unplanted form: with plants added to soften the outlines and edges, a raised-bed group of this sort can create a dynamic feature.

Raised beds can also perform a valuable linking or directional function in the design. Positioned either side of a doorway or garden gate, they will draw attention to it and help direct the eye to the place to walk through. And built along the edge of a lawn or terrace at the top of a steep slope, a long raised bed filled with plants marks the level change to provide a subliminal safety barrier.

Raising the height of the plantings can be a useful design element, whatever the size of the plot. Entire borders can be raised to help disguise boundary fences and walls, especially in small gardens where it can be difficult to create height in a limited space.

Here, rendered blockwork walls are stepped and staggered to provide a varied series of raised beds for ornamentals.

This integrated design incorporates seating atop the strong curve of the wall, with a simple water feature.

Bright colours can be used to make a feature of the structure and add a sense of fun to raised-bed gardens.

Building raised beds into sloping gardens is an ideal way to create level planting areas, which will also help to retain soil and prevent it washing away. Such terracing to form stepped raised beds not only makes planting and maintenance easier; it also makes more of the plants by presenting them to view at each of the changes in level. The area behind the retaining walls can then be backfilled with a good-quality soil-and-compost mix to provide the best growing conditions (see page 194).

Meanwhile, a whole range of other features, such as ponds, terraces, and steps, can be incorporated into retaining walls to form raised beds. This sort of built-in design makes for a more integrated appearance, particularly where there are lots of different levels in the plot.

Getting the dimensions right

The design of raised beds is strongly influenced by the types of plants that are to be grown in them. The height, spread, and rooting depth of plants all have a bearing on the depth of soil they need to thrive, and this in turn influences bed shape and style.

Choose your height

If growing woody trees, shrubs, and fruit bushes, bear in mind that their roots will naturally grow down into the ground in search of moisture. In addition, their height needs to be counterbalanced by deep roots that are held securely in position in the soil. This can be ideally accommodated where a raised bed is built above existing soil and so the supporting walls can be pretty much any height – from as little as 10cm (4in) to more than 1 metre (3¼ft) tall.

   If the bed is built on a solid base, however, such woody plants will need the deepest root run you can provide, which means a minimum of 80cm (31in). Of course, this means that any raised bed will need to be at least this tall.

   By contrast, shallow-rooting herbaceous perennials and biennials, annuals, and most summer vegetables can be grown in a shallower bed if necessary. Where used to retain an edge around an existing soil bed, it again need only be 10cm (4in) in height. On a solid base, a minimum depth of 30cm (12in) should be allowed, although deeper would be better. Where weight is an issue – for rooftop installations, for example (see page 132) – such shallow beds will help to minimize the load, but it is essential to seek advice from a structural engineer before going ahead.

Tall plants are given extra prominence in a high raised bed, flanked by lower beds and planting.

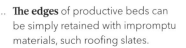

The edges of productive beds can be simply retained with impromptu materials, such roofing slates.

The tapering height of these beds creates a level planting surface on a slope, and an inviting path.

Medium-height plantings at the base of this raised bed provide a visual link to the shorter, upper-level plants around the base of a centrepiece Japanese maple.

Structural integrity

The taller the raised bed, the more structural integrity it will need in its walls to support not only its own height, but also the weight of the growing medium and the plants it contains. This will affect the materials chosen to build it from and the dimensions of the supporting walls themselves. It may be beneficial to include cross bracing between walls inside the bed to prevent the weight of the soil from pushing them apart.

Remember, too, that a tall bed can look dominant and imposing, particularly in a small, enclosed space such as a balcony or courtyard. However, there may be a necessity to overcome poor or non-existent soil, or to provide accessibility, so don't scrimp on height: instead, try to grade and blend individual beds into the overall design of your garden or growing space with associated structural planting around the edges to soften the appearance.

Size it right

For shallow, productive beds the practical aspects are most important in dictating their size. These are usually constructed simply to keep the soil in place and to create a level surface on which to grow. In this case, the height would usually be around 20cm (8in) but can be up to 90cm (35in) where mobility and access issues dictate.

As for width and length, such beds can be made to suit circumstances, but realistically they can't be less than 30cm (12in) wide or long to earn the name of raised bed and to warrant their construction. Smaller than this and pots or containers make a more economic option.

Normally, a minimum size might be 1 metre × 1 metre to create a bed suitable for metre-square growing (3ft × 3ft for foot-square growing in the US; see page 154 for details). For a longer, more conventional strip bed, a width of 60–70cm (24–28in) allows easy tending from each side, and a length of 1.2–1.6 metres (4–5ft) means you won't have a long walk to circumnavigate it. Where space allows, positioning consecutive rows or blocks of these beds, with a 40–50cm (16–20in) path between them, will optimize use of the ground while still allowing access between the beds for tending crops. Wheelchair access would warrant a path 1.2 metres (4ft) wide.

Meanwhile, narrow 30–40cm (12–16in) beds around the edges of the plot are useful for shade-tolerant species, climbing specimens, or wall-trained plants, which can make efficient use of the third, vertical dimension. Such a regular arrangement is convenient for organizing and growing veg, fruit, and cut-flower crops.

Similar minimum sizes can apply to ornamental raised beds. Both width and length may be governed by the ultimate spread of the plants you

Minimum sizes

As a guide, the minimum size dimensions for productive beds are as follows:

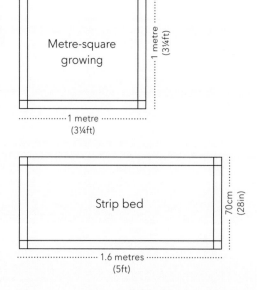

Metre-square growing

1 metre (3¼ft)

1 metre (3¼ft)

Strip bed

70cm (28in)

1.6 metres (5ft)

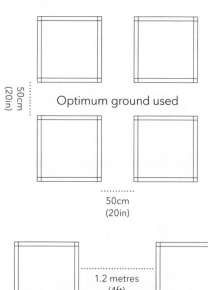

50cm (20in)

Optimum ground used

50cm (20in)

1.2 metres (4ft)

Wheelchair access

Big raised beds on paved surfaces hold a large volume of growing medium, essential for the long-term health of the plantings (top); held in place with timber edging, these shallow beds simply improve the depth and quality of pre-existing soil.

intend to grow, although pruning can be used to limit their size. Large shrubs, for example, might spread up to 1.4 metres (4½ft) across so a bed big enough to accommodate this is sensible. By contrast, diminutive alpine plants may be less than 10cm (4in) across, allowing a selection of different types to be grown in a bed of, say, 60cm × 60cm (24in × 24in).

Aesthetic design

As a rule, shallow and wide rectangular beds are most pleasing to the eye and should probably take up the majority of space in a raised-bed plot design. A few taller, cube-shaped beds can create a sense of height and provide contrast to the lower structures. However, don't be constrained by shape and remember that any bed or border that is planned in a garden design can be raised. The only limiting factor may be the cost of construction.

Volume to surface area

One of the most important considerations with designing a raised bed – in fact, with any sort of container growing – is the volume of soil that it contains. This is crucial to provide the plants with room to root and to use the growing medium to its full potential. The greater the volume, the better. After all, this is what generally happens in nature, or in the garden, where plants grow in the open soil with a pretty much unrestricted root run.

Root development

Small raised beds and containers will encourage roots to the edges, as this is where any water not only flows through first, but then quickly drains from. And as the water drains, it sucks in air containing oxygen, which is just as important as moisture for the health and growth of plant roots. Encouraged to the edge in this way, the roots will then circle round, without using the full volume of the soil or compost. By contrast, in larger beds and containers, water will tend to soak in more effectively over the surface of the growing medium, and plant roots will be less likely to grow out to the edges.

Tall raised beds allow a large volume of growing medium in proportion to their surface area, and thus enable plants to be grown more successfully where there is no underlying soil.

Moisture and temperature

The volume of soil in a raised bed can affect the amount of moisture in other ways, too, as well as the nutrients available, and the temperature of the rooting area. In a ground-level bed or border, the soil surface is the only way heat and cold can be transmitted, while in a raised bed the sides can warm and cool, too. This causes soil temperatures to fluctuate more readily, especially in small raised beds of minimal volume.

Solid paving or other surfaces can also radiate heat or cold into a raised bed to cause temperatures to range widely. Solid materials act like a storage heater to release heat over a prolonged period, and again, the effects are most pronounced in small, shallow beds.

In addition, small volumes of soil will lose moisture rapidly due to evaporation, either in hot, dry weather or when there is a strong, drying wind. This effect is compounded where beds are built onto an impermeable base, as there is no underlying reserve of moisture, which can move up through the soil by capillary action. And the greater the surface area of the bed in proportion to the volume of soil it contains, the more rapidly it will lose water. Bear in mind that tall beds drain very readily (unless filled with heavy soil) and there will be a reduction in capillary action allowing moisture to move up through the soil.

Plants lose moisture from their leaves, so benefit from having a large volume of soil or growing medium in which to root.

Add in evaporation of moisture from the plant leaves, which in turn is drawn in from the roots, and small volumes of soil can dry out in a matter of hours in hot weather.

So, although there are minimum depths and suggested widths and lengths for raised-bed growing, designing them to contain a large volume of soil is the best advice. And, where possible, build raised beds that are open at the base to the underlying garden soil to encourage deep rooting and to allow moisture to move up into the bed from the ground beneath.

Surface water loss

The amount of water loss from a raised bed depends on the ratio of surface area to volume, particularly when built on a solid surface. The two beds here, for example, both contain the same volume of soil, but the left one has a smaller surface area from which to lose moisture.

Deeper soil and smaller surface area means less evaporation and greater moisture retention.

Less evaporation

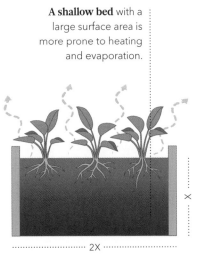

A shallow bed with a large surface area is more prone to heating and evaporation.

More evaporation

Harvest winter veg

Doris Kampas

In winter, my raised bed is particularly important for me, as I can get fresh vitamins from the garden into the kitchen every day. The raised-bed soil mix, the larch wood, and a cold frame attachment warm the vegetables and promote their growth even in cold temperatures, but to ensure a successful winter harvest, I also choose the right varieties of vegetables.

Doris Kampas lives in Austria, just outside Vienna. She is an agronomist and founder of the company bio-garten, which has been building raised beds from larch wood for its customers for more than 15 years. Together with BOKU Vienna (University of Natural Resources and Applied Life Sciences), bio-garten has studied the cultivation and irrigation of winter vegetables in raised beds. Doris is also the author of several books on raised beds.

   www.bio-garten.de
   Instagram: @biogarten

A winter veg bed can be colourful and architectural, as well as providing fresh produce through the season.

Winter vegetables are more diverse than you might think. In addition to the vegetables we are familiar with, such as spinach, lamb's lettuce, leeks, or kale, there are less common types, such as winter purslane, winter cress, staghorn plantain, or Asian vegetables. Some are particularly surprising, and you might not expect them to grow as winter vegetables in a raised bed. These include carrots, parsley, chard, beetroot, swede, radish, and various types of lettuce.

The taste of winter vegetables is sweet and very aromatic. The plants collect nutrients all year round and store them in autumn in the form of sugar compounds in their leaves, roots, and heads. They need the nutrients to have enough energy to form seeds and leaves after winter. In addition, the sugar serves as a natural antifreeze. Winter carrots are therefore much sweeter than summer carrots!

When growing winter vegetables, make sure you do it at the right time. Because although the vegetables are harvested in winter, they still need to be grown in the warm season in order to germinate and develop. Sowing or planting winter vegetables starts in spring (for example, parsnips), summer (for example, leeks), or autumn (for example, Asian vegetables), depending on the species.

PLANT LIST

This 1 metre × 2 metres (3¼ft × 6½ft) bed contains my favourite winter vegetables. I sow a row of parsnips thinly as early as March. In May I plant three Brussels sprouts plants and seven leek seedlings from mid-June. The rest of the vegetables – lettuce, winter purslane, and a colourful mix of Asian vegetables – are sown in September. The winter vegetables in my raised bed can tolerate frost down to -20°C (-4°F). However, the harvest must only take place on frost-free days so as not to damage the vegetables.

Brussels sprouts × 3
Cut-and-come-again lettuce
   'Misticanza' mix
Leeks × 7
Pak choi × 4
Winter purslane × 8
Asian mustard greens, e.g.
   'Osaka Purple', 'Nine Headed Bird',
   'Green in Snow', 'Golden Frills',
   'Dragon's Tongue'
Parsnips × 4

Sow pak choi, and other hardy Asian vegetables, in September for an autumn or winter harvest.

Leeks are extremely hardy and will continue to grow during any mild spells of winter weather.

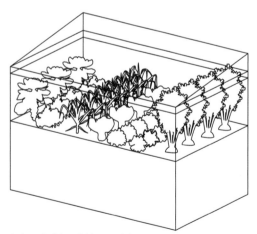

A detachable cold frame "lid" helps to keep winter crops growing and frost-free when temperatures really dip.

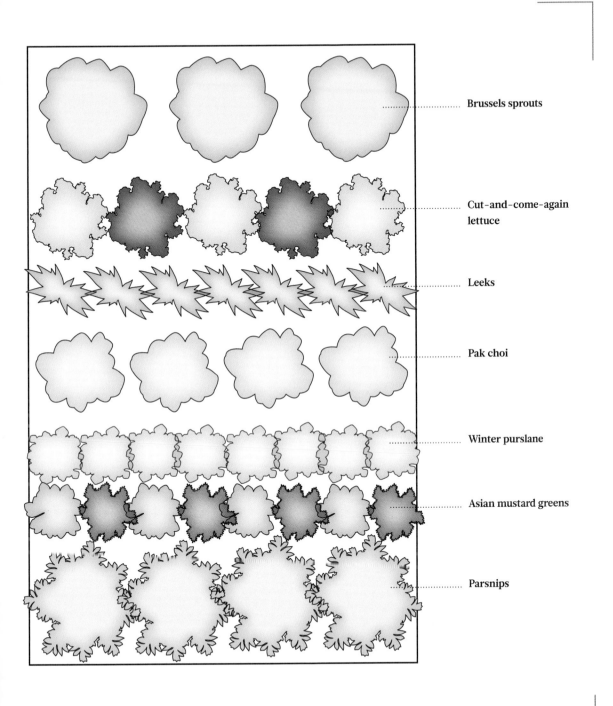

Brussels sprouts

Cut-and-come-again lettuce

Leeks

Pak choi

Winter purslane

Asian mustard greens

Parsnips

Hollow walls

Low walls can be transformed into a growing space and a decorative feature by building them with two parallel faces, with a soil-filled gap between. This, in effect, forms a narrow raised bed, which can be used to grow alpines, compact ornamentals, and even low hedging to make an attractive boundary.

Mind the gap

Where possible, it is worth making the space between the two wall faces at least 30cm (12in) wide to provide a good volume of soil and plenty of rooting room. The benefit of leaving a wider gap is that any foundations to support mortared brick or stone walls can be dug individually, and soil added in between them. If this is well forked through and improved by the addition of some organic matter, it will allow roots to grow down into the ground below and the wall to drain effectively.

Hollow walls can also be built of drystone (without mortar joints), timber, or metal. Bear in mind, however, that the latter can readily transmit heat and cold into the soil, which can stress, damage, or kill plant roots, especially where only a narrow strip of infill soil is used.

The height can be 20cm–1 metre (8in–3¼ft), but the taller the hollow wall, the more free-draining it will be. Building such a structure above 1 metre (3¼ft) is generally impractical for both plant growth and construction, so for taller walls it is best to make the base a solid construction and start the hollow wall in the top 50cm (20in) to create a deep planting trough. But remember that maintenance might be an issue above 1.5 metres (5ft) tall.

Such walls provide a great home for succulents such as creeping sedums, as well as alpine phlox and aubrieta. They can also be used for herbs, including thyme, marjoram, and oregano.

Boundary walls can incorporate planting spaces within them to soften their appearance and provide additional growing space.

Creative terracing

Sloping gardens provide plenty of opportunity for terracing using retaining walls, the main aim of this being to create level areas for cultivation.

In essence, terracing creates half a raised bed behind each retaining wall running across the slope, and usually involves an element of cut and fill where soil is "cut" out from the bank and used to "fill" further down.

This reduces the amount of soil that needs to be brought in for the scheme; however, if the soil is poor (heavy clay, very sandy, or filled with rubble) then walls can be simply built at intervals up the slope. Ideally, the top of the lowest wall will be level with the base of the next and so on. And then each layer can be filled level with a good-quality topsoil mixture to create the terraces.

Different on every level

However they are formed, the broad level beds of soil will tend to be more free-draining and drier behind the top of each wall and wetter at the foot. This in turn will dictate the plants that can be grown, as well as their performance, in contrast to the broadly uniform conditions found in a free-standing raised bed.

On steep sites, growing conditions will also be affected by the aspect of the terraces. This means the direction that they face, whether north, south, east, or west, or degrees of the compass in between. The capacity for the terrace walls to cast shade or to be exposed to the heating effects of the sun, among other factors, can create subtle microclimates, which will alter the way plants are able to grow.

123

Containers as raised beds

Anything that contains soil above the usual ground level could be considered a raised bed. In their moveable form, these include containers, planters, and, at the smallest scale, pots.

The most important prerequisite of all of these is that they have some means by which excess water can drain out of the growing medium so that the plant roots don't become waterlogged and die.

Ready-made raised beds

At the largest scale, containers or planters can provide a sufficient volume of good-quality soil or growing medium for multiple plants. In essence,

each one is a small raised bed, subject to all the climate and growing influences discussed earlier in this chapter. For the same reasons as for raised beds, the larger the container, the greater the volume of soil and the more consistent the growing conditions will be. Ideally, they should be a minimum of 45cm (18in) in diameter and depth to help retain moisture at the roots and minimize any plant stress.

Grouping individual containers close together, even butting them up tightly next to one another, will help insulate the soil from extremes of heat and cold. This in turn will prevent the soil from drying out quickly and help protect plant roots.

Constructing with containers

Particularly creative is the use of large containers and pots to create "plantable" walls for raised beds or terraces. Cube-shaped pots and troughs can be packed and stacked easily on a firm, level base, and then filled with good-quality soil. Alternatively, you can cement large conventional flowerpots in place, filling the gaps between them with mortared stone or brick to make a retaining wall. This method could be used to create a feature wall, with the less visible sides built of more conventional materials.

Containers can be grouped and stacked to make retaining walls for raised beds.

Recycled and re-loved, a galvanized metal bath makes an ideal improvised bed.

Trough beds

As the name implies, trough beds are usually as wide as they are deep, and of variable lengths. They take inspiration from feeding troughs used in animal husbandry on farms.

You can make trough beds using off-the-shelf agricultural troughs (adding plenty of drainage holes in the base), or purpose-build them from timber, brick, or stone. Generally, they have square sides, which means that the volume of soil remains consistent throughout their depth. As with hollow walls, the wider the trough, the better the root run – a minimum width of 30cm (12in) and depth of 45cm (18in) is preferable.

From the farmyard to the garden

Well suited to small gardens, long, narrow troughs are ideal for positioning around the boundaries of a plot. However, they can also be accommodated in parallel blocks to provide easily accessible planting space. This is particularly useful for growing vegetable, herb, and cut-flower crops.

In the same way as pots and containers, you can use troughs to form the supporting walls of a raised bed and provide some cultivable space. In addition, you can stand them on the tops of walls forming terraces, or along the edge of a terrace or balcony.

Filled with lightweight compost and perlite for drainage, troughs and large individual containers may allow for raised-bed cultivation on roof gardens as long as their filled and wet weight is considered, and proper load-bearing calculations are carried out by a structural surveyor.

At their smallest, trough beds can make window boxes, though these usually have very limited volume to contain a growing medium. Filled with a gritty soil mix, they are most suitable for growing succulent species such as aeoniums, echeverias, and a wide variety of sedums.

Herb spirals and towers

Raised above the natural ground level, raised beds tend to have sharp drainage, and for many herbs that is a great benefit. However, not all herbs thrive in dry conditions and building a simple herb spiral or tower can provide various degrees of moisture to cater for their requirements.

Gardening in tiers

Creating a number of different layers in your herb tower, stacked one on top of the other, will allow water to drain progressively from the topmost level down through the lower ones, where moisture will be retained for longer. And by making the lower levels larger than those at the top, the greater volume of soil will also help to hold on to water and provide a cooler root run.

A spiral structure built with rocks is probably one of the simplest forms of raised bed, built around a mound of gritty soil. Equally straightforward is to create a layered tower of containers, starting with

a large one at the base and getting progressively smaller towards the top. Each one is half filled with the soil mixture and firmed, before nesting the next container inside – rather in the style of matryoshka or stacking dolls.

Another alternative is to use one large container or raised bed at the base and set large pots into the soil mix at different heights to provide subtle differences in moisture-holding. The pots that sit out of the soil the most will provide the best drainage and warmest summer root run, while those set deeper into the bed will stay moister and cooler.

126

Stacks and pyramids

Creating layered planting makes effective use of water in raised beds, particularly during hot, dry weather, but it also makes efficient use of space. Taking your growing to the third dimension is particularly useful in small plots or on a balcony where space is at a premium.

Multi-layered planting

Simple stacking – creating progressively smaller raised beds, one on top of the other – does not increase the flat growing surface area, but the edges of each level allow a certain amount of plant overhang when planted immediately behind the top of the wall. This is of practical benefit when growing herbs, vegetables, and fruit.

With careful planning and positioning of each crop, space can be used to its best advantage – low-growing and trailing plants at the uppermost layers, and taller ones grown at the base of the walls on each layer so that they don't shade others. Those plants that need more moisture can be planted in the lower beds where water will drain down from the higher levels.

The design of such a multi-layer bed will depend on the growing space available and the position of the sun. In an open position, a pyramid can be created, stepped on each side. This can be built with each layer in the same orientation, or with alternate layers at 45 degrees to the previous one. However, where the bed is built against a wall or fence, or in a position that is in deep shade from one aspect, then a one-sided stepped design may be more appropriate.

Add grit or coarse sand to the growing mixture in the upper levels of layered plantings to allow moisture to drain away from the crowns of plants that relish dry conditions.

The compartmentalized sections of a pyramid bed can be planted with the same crop, or the soil mix tailored to suit the needs of different plants.

Crate garden

There are a whole host of impromptu materials and containers that can be used to make raised beds, but recycling plastic or wooden crates to plant into provides the grower with real flexibility.

Ideally, multiple crates of a standard size should be used so that they can be packed together efficiently with no gaps in between. These are then lined with a geotextile material, hessian sacking, layers of cardboard, or old carpet, before filling them with a growing medium. Thus, each crate becomes a planting "unit" or container.

Reuse, repot, rearrange

While many types of raised beds are permanent structures, a crate garden allows for the individual units to be swapped in and out – whether to change seasonal displays of ornamentals or to replace harvested veg plants with a fresh batch of seedlings for a succession of crops.

Such a tightly grouped collection of multiple planters makes, in effect, a single raised bed so could be surrounded by a "frame" wall of timber, stone, or brick for a neat visual effect. This will have the added advantage of insulating the outside edge of the crates from excess heat and cold or preventing them from drying out. Meanwhile, the inner crates will provide protection for each other.

Where space allows, you can move crates that contain seasonal bulbs or other ornamentals to a less prominent position where they can continue to grow or die back naturally, then bring them back into the display "bed" the following season. When growing vegetables, you can sow, plant up, and grow on batches of seedlings and young plants in the wings, ready to move them to their final growing position as required.

Recycled wooden crates make ideal containers that can be grouped and interchanged for raised-bed growing.

Tyre garden

Reusable materials come in all shapes and sizes, and particularly useful are those that are robust and long lasting, such as vehicle tyres. They have become a popular means of making a raised bed, either singly or stacked two to four high.

Tyres can also be used to create the outer walls of a larger raised bed: used in this way the internal diameter of the tyres can be filled with different topsoil mixes, if required, to create bespoke planting pockets around the edges for different plants. They also make a good walling material to create shallow terraces on gently sloping ground, again creating planting pockets to increase stability and provide useful raised growing space.

A hard-working material

The density of the rubber used to make tyres means that they help insulate the bed from any winter cold, but their black colour means they can also absorb energy from the sun to warm the soil for early crops when growing vegetables. Meanwhile, their impact resistance and lack of sharp edges makes them good for building raised beds to accommodate wheelchair access and for children's gardens.

If they can be sourced, lorry or tractor tyres are large enough to create individual raised beds and those with deep or ribbed tread patterns can look very artistic. They're great to use as a centrepiece or focal point in a garden design and are robust enough to provide an edge to sit on.

Durable and long-lasting, tyres can be used singly or stacked to make retaining walls for raised beds.

Hot beds

Historically, raised hot beds played a big part in producing exotic crops such as pineapples and melons in the gardens of wealthy landowners, but they also offer a great way to boost early cropping in cool, temperate climates.

This useful horticultural technique relies on the heat generated by decomposing manure to warm the soil. And if this is covered with a cold frame, the warmth can be trapped in the air above the soil to keep temperatures 5°C (41°F) (or more) higher than the outdoor temperature, depending on prevailing weather conditions. The bed can be used to raise early batches of seedlings and plants. Built in mid-winter, it would be particularly useful for seasonal crops such as beetroot, lettuce, carrots, salad onions, spinach, chard, radishes, and turnips.

Get digging

There are a number of different ways of creating such a hot bed, but one of the best methods, if space allows, is to excavate a pit in the ground, about 50cm (20in) deep and at least 1 metre (3¼ft) square. This is then overfilled with fresh horse or cattle manure, compacted in layers, creating a mound that can extend up to 30cm (12in) above ground. The benefit of burying part of the heap in the ground is that it will help to retain heat. The edges of the heap can be held in place with a 50cm (20in) high timber framework of planks, corrugated sheets, or straw bales to form a raised bed. If built on a solid base, the sides of the bed can be around 1 metre (3¼ft) tall to retain the whole heap above ground.

Finally, the manure is levelled off and topped with 15–20cm (6–8in) of topsoil mix, and the walls of the bed are used to support a frame glazed with glass, Perspex, or a polythene sheet to trap the warmth, while allowing daylight to penetrate.

Once used for early-season crops, the warm, rich soil can then be sown or planted with tender summer crops such as tomatoes, peppers, aubergines, and squashes.

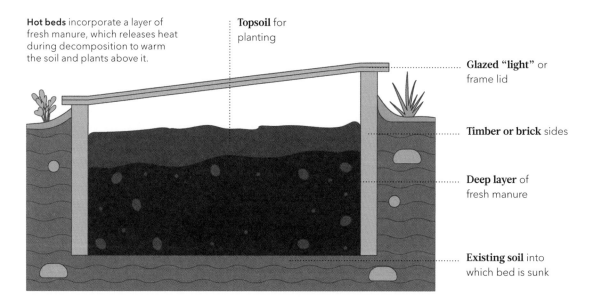

Hot beds incorporate a layer of fresh manure, which releases heat during decomposition to warm the soil and plants above it.

Topsoil for planting

Glazed "light" or frame lid

Timber or brick sides

Deep layer of fresh manure

Existing soil into which bed is sunk

Table-top growing

Lifted off the ground on legs, table beds or raised troughs provide a moveable and flexible option for small growing spaces.

The ultimate raised bed is one that is completely lifted off the ground to create a "growing table". These structures are not only useful when floor space is at a premium; they also help overcome various access and mobility challenges.

A growing table usually takes the form of a large trough with base and sides, raised and supported on legs so that the finished surface will be approximately 90cm (35in) above the ground. Such a structure is great for small spaces and where there is no access to soil at ground level. It is suitable for seasonal vegetables, strawberries, and herbs, as well as annual, biennial, and perennial flowers. And by being lifted up, the bed is made suitable for older gardeners, those with restricted mobility, and children.

Elevate your planting
Off-the-shelf modules are widely available, but they are also easy to build from timber or metal. Ideally, the trough should be a minimum of 30cm (12in) deep to provide a good volume of soil to grow in. The width should be no more than 1.2 metres (4ft)

when it can be accessed from both sides, but only up to 60cm (24in) if one side is positioned against a wall or fence. Ultimately, it can be any length that you require.

Such a bed will be reliant on the gardener to provide regular watering during dry weather, even during periods of cool temperatures. And, as with any container, make sure it has good provision for drainage to stop the growing medium from becoming waterlogged.

Most usefully, raising plants in this way and virtually disconnecting them from the ground could have some benefits when it comes to pests and diseases. Slugs and snails, for example, may be less likely to crawl up the legs to graze on crops and other plants, while increased air circulation under and around the elevated bed can be useful in reducing the incidence of fungal infection.

Adding growing space to roofs

Creating green roofs on all types of buildings is recognized as being of huge benefit to the environment and in combatting both the causes and outcomes of climate change. In effect, in many cases the growing medium and the plants are retained on a roof by means of a raised bed.

Growing green

At its shallowest, this kind of raised bed can be little more than a system of frames 6-8cm (2¼-3in) deep to support mat-forming, drought-resistant sedums. An increased depth of 10-15cm (4-6in) can support a wide range of grass and turf species, while deeper-rooting herbaceous plants and even shrubs and trees will require a minimum of 30cm (12in) to thrive. This latter depth also makes it possible to grow a wide range of herbs, vegetables, and even fruit to create a productive roof. In all cases it is crucial to check the load bearing of the roof with a structural engineer before installation.

Perhaps unexpectedly, the soil in a green roof offers good insulation – against both heat and cold. And adding plants into the mix adds a further level of protection, with their foliage naturally absorbing some of the sun's energy while trapping pockets of air between their leaves, which reduces temperature fluctuations. All of this can improve the energy efficiency of our homes by reducing the need for heating and air conditioning.

Even the smallest roofs on sheds and bin stores can be topped off with a green roof. They will have the benefit of slowing rainwater run-off and stabilizing temperatures in the garden environment. But what is often overlooked are the added visual and psychological benefits of the colour green itself, which will soften the appearance of garden structures and help improve mental wellbeing.

On a roof, beds need to be filled with a lightweight growing medium and are best planted with species that can cope with dry, high-light conditions.

Wall-mounted growing space

With raised beds, as with so many other things in life, it sometimes pays to think outside the box – well, the horizontal box in any case. And by reimagining their supporting function into the vertical axis, it is possible to clothe walls and other upright surfaces with ornamental or productive growing space.

Small, wall-mounted "raised beds" optimize productive or decorative space in the tightest of growing places.

Growing up

Green walls help us to use space effectively and, like green roofs, make a significant contribution to softening the built environment, as well as insulating buildings and ameliorating temperature extremes in gardens. This is particularly useful in small gardens and courtyards as well as on balconies, where there is proportionately more vertical space. Green walls can also be created indoors.

The simplest means of taking advantage of this third dimension is to use multiple narrow troughs or window boxes, mounted on brackets attached to walls, fences, or trellis panels. Try positioning these one above another, with space between to allow foliage to grow up and then spill out. In the same way, you could incorporate troughs into a free-standing screen supported by a couple of end posts.

There are also a number of different green-wall modular systems available commercially. Most of these take the form of a shallow box, with distinct planting holes. Such designs allow the whole structure to be filled with a lightweight growing medium and then planted up while it is lying flat on the ground. Having been grown on in this orientation for a few weeks, ideally, to get good root establishment and stabilization, one or more modules are then lifted into the vertical position and attached to their supports.

A drip irrigation system is usually an intrinsic part of making such growing a success.

Table-top treats

Patrick Vernuccio

As a balcony gardener, I'm growing all my vegetables, fruits, and herbs in pots and containers. Raised beds are definitely playing an essential role in this food production, because compared to pots, they offer a greater soil volume capacity, allowing gardeners to harvest more, and also to experience the benefits of companion planting.

Rows of radishes make for a colourful bed that is both edible and ornamental.

Patrick Vernuccio, aka "The Frenchie Gardener", is a French author, facilitator, and content creator on urban balcony gardening. He shares his deep passion for growing food in small urban spaces and educates over one million people on his social media accounts. Patrick advocates welcoming nature back into our cities and our lives, to recreate this essential connection with food, seasons, and biodiversity.

www.thefrenchiegardener.com
Instagram: @thefrenchiegardener
YouTube: @thefrenchiegardener

On a balcony, terrace, or patio, floor space is scarce and precious, so you need to come up with clever solutions to grow vertically, optimizing the growing space. That is why I'm mostly using raised beds in the form of a grow table. They are elevated on legs, which saves floor space for storage and other pots. It also helps to protect plants from our crawling friends, slugs and snails!

Raised beds are also the perfect tool to grow crops across all four seasons. When filled at the start of the growing year with a healthy potting mix, manure, and pulped food scraps from bokashi composting, this soil has a rich, long-lasting quality, which allows nutrients to diffuse slowly to the plants. Then, you only have to plan and implement crop rotations, without having to fully replace the soil.

An important consideration when planting in these grow-table raised beds is not to overcrowd them. Maintaining good spacing between varieties is key, so that plants have enough space to develop healthy roots below the ground, but also enough horizontal space for the foliage to grow above the ground. I always prioritize quality over quantity.

I also add a mulch in the form of straw or grass clippings. This helps to save precious water during summer, but also keep the soil warmer in winter.

PLANT LIST

These grow-table designs measure L80cm × H70cm × D35cm (L31in × H28in × D14in). They are diverse, space efficient, and applicable across our four seasons, even if you just have a very small balcony. This grow table has a soil volume capacity of 50 litres, and you can even attach pots of 3–4 litres to the table legs via a cable clamp or some twine to welcome herbs to the mix. For spring/summer, you can maintain a long supply of lettuce by harvesting it leaf by leaf. You can also plant radishes and replant new ones every month and a half. For autumn/winter, I usually start my seedlings of kale, turnips, and spinach in the third week of August to replant in mid-September. All these are frost hardy to -10°C (14°F) without protection.

Spring/summer
Lettuce × 4
Radish × 30
Sage
Mint
Basil

Autumn/winter
Kale × 2
Spinach 'Giant Winter' × 2
Turnips × 4
Rosemary
Coriander
Parsley

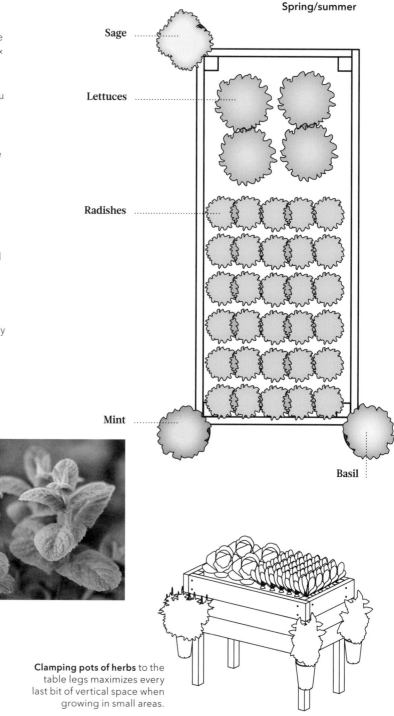

Spring/summer

Sage

Lettuces

Radishes

Mint

Basil

Clamping pots of herbs to the table legs maximizes every last bit of vertical space when growing in small areas.

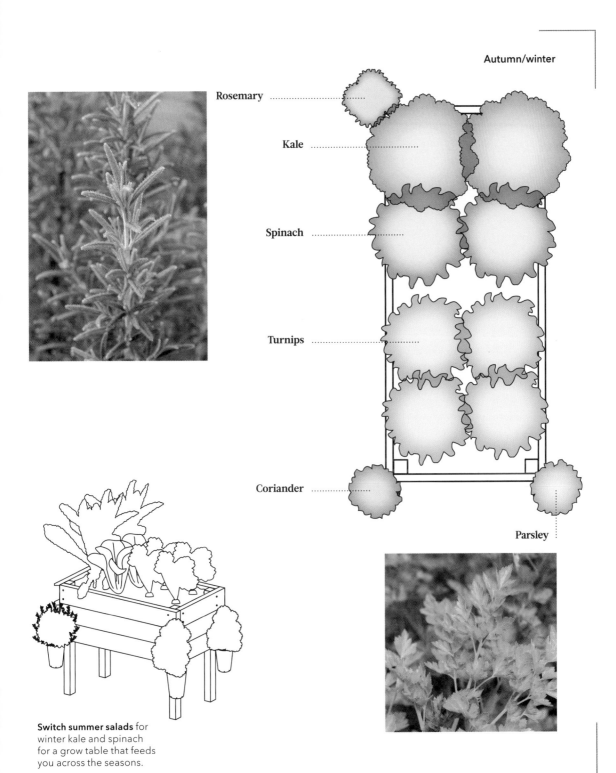

Rosemary

Kale

Spinach

Turnips

Coriander

Parsley

Switch summer salads for winter kale and spinach for a grow table that feeds you across the seasons.

How to build

Level the land

Raising the growing level on flat ground is what most of us regard as creating raised beds, but when it comes to the practicalities of construction, not all gardens, plots, or even balconies are created level.

Get it straight

It pays to check the whole area before building or installing a ready-made structure to get a feel for the overall levels you're working with. It is irritating to live with a structure that is slightly out of true. In fact, if something is a little out of alignment, it is often much more obvious once the structure is built, when there is plenty of time to sit, reflect, and consider the outcome.

Use a straight-edged length of timber and a spirit level to check for any slope or "fall" in the ground and, based on the size of bed you want to construct, work out how much the difference will be both end to end and across the width of the bed. If it is less than 5mm (¼in), it is unlikely that it will be noticed, especially if there are no level walls, fences, or other structures close by to reference it against.

Having one side of the bed lower than the other can, in fact, prove an advantage in some instances. While the main aim of creating raised beds and terraces is to retain soil and produce a broadly level surface to plant into, a slight slope towards the sun at midday can help to warm the soil and allow more even light penetration into crops or plants in temperate, high-latitude parts of the world. If such a slope is desirable, aim to make it gentle – not more than a 1:10 gradient – to reduce the chances of the soil "creeping" or moving down the slope.

Where a level growing surface is required for a free-standing raised bed, slight slopes in the existing ground can usually be taken into account during the building process. When constructing on a solid path or base, any difference can be accommodated by packing or filling the lower side to raise its level. If making the bed on open ground, then a good alternative to this is to dig out the soil on the higher side to create a level site on which to construct the bed.

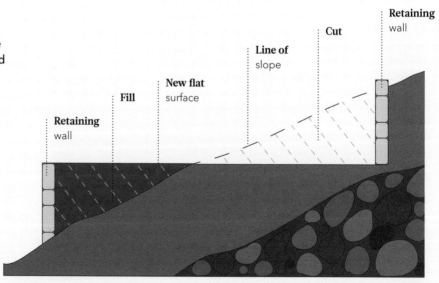

Cut and fill

This "cut and fill" technique takes excess soil from the upper slope to build up the lower end, transforming the ground into level terraced beds.

Retaining wall

Fill

New flat surface

Line of slope

Cut

Retaining wall

Retaining wall

Reducing the slope of the ground will help to prevent soil washing away in heavy rain.

> "If making the bed on open ground then dig out the soil on the higher side to create a level site on which to construct the bed"

Terraced beds

A subtle adaptation of a free-standing raised bed can be used for plots with slopes of a 1:5 gradient or more. This effectively takes the form of terracing, where excess soil is excavated and used to fill behind a retaining wall lower down the slope. This is usually referred to as "cut and fill", and each layer creates, in effect, a raised bed, albeit raised only on one side.

The retaining walls in each case will be holding back, or "retaining", a large weight of soil – particularly if they are more than 30cm (12in) tall – and will need to be built on good foundations. We'll look in more detail at the sorts of foundations or supports that may be needed as this chapter unfolds, specifically with regards to the materials the walls or beds are to be built from and their size.

Try to limit the number of terraces cut into a slope. Lots of little terraces can look fussy and can make it difficult to keep the ground secure.

Off the shelf or bespoke?

Ready-made kits might be the easier option, but building a raised bed in situ can optimize space to suit your needs.

Pre-made for you

Many home growers choose to buy a commercially produced raised-bed kit or preassembled unit for ease. Unsurprisingly, this means there is a huge amount of choice out there in a range of designs and styles, made from lots of different materials.

Simple kits include pre-cut timber, metal, and plastic beds with screws and fittings supplied to put them together. They require relatively simple tools and, in some cases, these are provided in the kit, too. Here the main consideration is convenience, and most companies offer a range of sizes, which should suit the majority of standard situations. You can also use beds of different dimensions creatively to put together a unified scheme of levels and growing spaces. However, these kits rarely offer good value for money when compared with what can be made by buying the raw materials.

Raised containers

Other commercial raised beds include folding metal or wooden frames, which support some form of container for growing in. Lightweight and easy to store in winter, they are aimed at balcony and courtyard growers, but are too small to hold enough compost or topsoil to be of real benefit to the plants growing in them. Realistically, many of these products may only last one or two growing seasons, and barely deserve the name "raised bed".

Table beds

Moving up the scale, there are also a number of different tabletop-style raised-bed systems available. These take the form of a large, lined trough supported on legs (see page 131). Most are robust and well finished. Timber is invariably used in their construction, and they may be delivered ready-made or in pre-made sections for easy self-assembly with just a few tools. There are also plastic products on the market, which don't rot, but they need checking to ensure that they are made from UV-stabilized material so that they won't become brittle with exposure to sunlight.

A benefit of some of these models is the range of accessories available to go with them, from specially tailored mesh and net covers to protect plants from certain pests and diseases, to folding plastic cloches that fit snugly over the top of the bed to divert excess rain and provide a little frost protection. Some come with integrated watering systems, too, which aim to make growing easier.

These products are convenient and do offer a way in to growing plants in raised beds, particularly where there is limited space available. Plus, they are a great way to get children into gardening.

Self-assembly raised beds can be easily bolted together so you can get growing quickly.

Large containers are, in effect, raised beds, in which a wide range of plants can be grown.

Do-it-yourself

Most successful growing spaces, whatever their size, have an element of design, and when coupled with the fact that no two gardens – or the requirements of the gardener – are exactly alike, building beds to fit the space undoubtedly seems the ideal option.

This is particularly so in oddly shaped plots, where you can tailor your project to make the best use of space. It is also preferable where a specific style or look is required to suit the house and its surroundings. When there are specific access and use requirements, such a made-to-measure approach has huge benefits.

The cost of this approach varies widely according to the materials you choose for the build – after all, the results can range from a simple timber construction (see page 148) to pretty much anything your heart desires.

Self-build skills are not beyond the average DIY enthusiast, and there is lots of advice in this book. However, if there is a reliance on the supply of special materials or availability of craftworkers and builders, it could result in the scheme taking a while to be measured, planned, and built, meaning that it could be months or even years before growing can get underway. And without careful budgeting, more elaborate, built-in schemes could prove very costly.

Working with different materials

When it comes to choosing what to use to build raised beds, there are pros and cons to be considered with each material, to understand the best way to build with them. Fundamentally, it comes down to affordability and practicality, as well as personal taste.

The latter will often dictate the style and design from the outset. Creating something that suits the garden, balcony, or indoor environment may be important to the homeowner, and this will depend to a large extent on the fabric of the building. A raised bed built from stone that is in keeping with a traditionally built house, for example, is often thought of as desirable, but stark contrasts may be considered more modern and stylish (see Chapter 3, page 99).

In certain circumstances there may be local authority planning considerations to take into account as well, which is more likely in high-profile locations – such as front gardens – and where an existing building or even the garden is listed. All these considerations will affect what you decide to build your raised bed from.

Where there are no such restrictions, and if design and style considerations are unimportant to the homeowner, then decisions about what to use can be made based on more practical matters, such as cost, availability, ease of construction, durability, and maintenance.

Bear in mind, also, that raised beds and other constructions usually last for many years. You will have to live with the choices you make about what to build them from for the long term. And don't forget that materials will change in appearance with age – some may improve like a fine wine, others may deteriorate.

Quick and easy-to-fix timber

Wood is probably the first thing that springs to mind for containing soil around the edges of a border or for using to build a more substantial raised bed. It can take many forms, from rough-sawn and planed timber from the builder's merchant or timber yard, through to sawn log sections. In addition, there is the opportunity to use railway sleepers (both new and recycled), and timber palisade stakes, as well as reclaimed pallet wood or scaffold boards.

Suitability

Timber is available in two basic types – softwood or hardwood. The former is harvested from quick-growing forestry trees (usually conifers), which have a wide grain (space between the annual growth rings) and therefore tend to be lightweight. Heavier hardwoods mostly have a narrow grain, which makes them denser but they tend to take longer to grow before harvesting.

Softwood timber is considerably cheaper than its hardwood relative, as well as being more flexible. And while it contains lots of natural oils and terpenes that go some way to preserving it, the coarser grain of the wood makes it more prone to rotting. Much of the timber for outdoor use is pressure treated with preservative to reduce the risk of rotting and, in some cases, to prevent pest infestation, too.

Wood transmits both heat and cold very slowly. This makes it a good insulator and great for use around the roots of plants to protect them from the heating effects of the sun in summer and the penetration of cold and frost in winter. And it surely goes without saying that the thicker the timber, the more efficiently it insulates.

It is also slightly porous, even in its preservative-treated form, which means that it can absorb and transmit water. Plus, any joints are unlikely to be so close fitting as to prevent water seeping between them. Such absorbency does make wood more prone to rotting, particularly when preservatives break down through weathering or the heat of the sun. Regular ongoing maintenance is therefore required to keep wood in good condition.

Timber is also relatively lightweight in proportion to its strength, as well as being quick and easy to build with. It is comparatively cheap to buy, too, and to pay for a tradesperson to construct with.

Naturalistic plantings
associate well with timber, especially these weathered railway sleepers.

Seating can be easily incorporated into the side walls of timber raised beds. The materials are relatively lightweight, too – an important consideration on a rooftop installation.

Timber raised beds associate well with areas of decking, helping to create a unified look to the overall design of a garden.

Used vertically, railway sleepers can be stepped in height to accommodate sloping sides to a raised bed.

Built with screws, a wooden raised bed can be readily dismantled if necessary or reconfigured as you require.

Lastly, it is sustainable when obtained from certified sources – for example, those approved by the Forest Stewardship Council (FSC) in the UK – as new trees can be planted to replace those used for timber. Plus it is biodegradable when it comes to the end of its useful life – though hopefully that won't happen too soon, if treated with environmentally friendly wood preservatives.

Tips for building with timber

Sleepers: Sleepers offer a good alternative to conventional sawn and planed timber planks. The original timber sleepers used in railway construction are available in limited quantities from salvage yards and specialist suppliers. However, these will have been treated over their years of use with tar and timber preservatives, which means they are dirty, tough to cut, and can leach chemicals into the soil that may be toxic to plants.

New sleepers, cut to similar dimensions to original railway sleepers, are widely available from timber merchants and online, and these are treated

with the same preservatives as standard timber planks. A number of companies produce "mini" sleepers in a range of sizes, some with a rectangular cross section, others with curved sides to create decorative effects.

The large cross-sectional dimensions of sleepers gives them useful stability for building raised beds and their sizes makes for quick construction. A single layer laid flat on the ground will have enough weight to retain an infill of topsoil and hold itself in place. Corner posts should be used to keep them secure when more than one "course" or layer is built up. Such posts can be dug into the ground and held in place with concrete. The sleepers are best drilled and secured to the posts using large-gauge coach screws, which usually have a square or hexagonal head for tightening in place with a spanner or socket set. For long beds, use intermediate posts to hold the sides in place.

Posts and palisades: While most timber-built beds use planks or sleepers laid horizontally, a different look can be created using timber posts installed vertically. Round or square posts can be employed: the former will give an informal palisade effect, while the latter creates a more stylish, modern look.

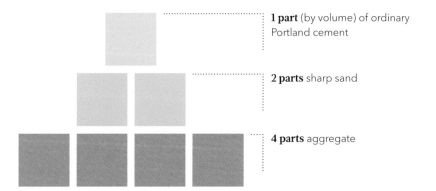

Concrete mix for posts

Bags of ready-mixed post-fixing concrete are available in standard and rapid-set formulations. Alternatively, it can be mixed on-site from:

Mix the dry cement, sand, and aggregate together thoroughly, before adding water, a little at a time, to make a stiff mix that holds its shape.

1 part (by volume) of ordinary Portland cement

2 parts sharp sand

4 parts aggregate

Buy timber that has been pressure-treated with preservative to ensure durability.

Log sections can also be used to make low-rise, informal bed edgings. These are best at least 25cm (10in) in diameter and approximately 25cm (10in) in height. Taller beds can be created with longer logs, but again these are best held in place in a shallow trench of concrete.

Maintenance

Any garden structure will need to be looked after to ensure it lasts as long as possible, and a raised bed is no exception. Not only does it need to repay the time and money you invested to build it in the first place, but its life needs to be extended to minimize any environmental impacts of its construction.

Wood is probably the most prone to decay of any material used. Pressure-treated when new, outdoor construction timber will be exposed to weathering by rain and sun, causing the protective oils to leach out. This will then leave the wood vulnerable to attack by decomposing fungi, which will cause it to decay – a particular problem on the inside of a timber structure or at the base where it comes into contact with moist soil. A whole host of insects also make it their mission to feed on the unprotected timber.

Round in section, "peeled and pointed" posts or stakes are a cheap-to-produce forestry product and are available in different lengths. The point at one end can be used to drive them vertically into the soil with a sledgehammer or post-driver. Add a minimum of half the height of the finished bed to the length of the posts, knocking this much into the ground to hold it in place. Do not exceed 50cm (20in) in bed height as the weight of the soil will tend to push the posts over.

Alternatively, dig a trench foundation and use a concrete mix (see opposite) to "haunch" the vertical posts in position. This method can also be used for square-section posts.

In all cases, brace the inside of the posts with horizontal lengths of timber, a minimum of 5cm × 5cm (2in × 2in) in section, screwing each one in position to provide additional support for the bed sides. Aim to use one horizontal brace for every 30cm (12in) of bed height.

Using preservatives

- Timber preservatives are generally water-, oil-, or solvent-based and should always be applied strictly in accordance with the manufacturer's instructions.
- Make sure that any wood preservative is appropriate to use on timber that comes into contact with plant material, to ensure it doesn't affect the health of the plants themselves and can't be taken up by edible crops.
- Check for any environmental impacts with regards to water, pollinators, and other vulnerable forms of life.
- There are standards for timber preservation and treatment in place. In the UK this is covered in the British Standard code of practice BS8417, which requires that the loading and penetration of preservative, impregnated into the wood, is tailored to the desired end use.
- Take care to use gloves and any other safety equipment, such as face masks and protective clothing, when applying chemical products.

Basic timber raised bed

A simple raised bed is easy to construct from low-cost timber or the wood from recycled pallets. Adapting this basic design will allow you to build a range of bed sizes and heights in straight-sided geometric shapes.

For ease of construction and economy, building a retaining box structure out of timber is a great way to make a raised bed. Either off-the-shelf "sawn" (unfinished) or "planed" timber can be used, depending on the desired look – the latter being more expensive and unnecessary for a utilitarian workhorse of a bed.

The construction method of the raised bed shown here is straightforward and, with care, it should be within the capability of anyone with basic tool skills.

Corner posts and planks for the sides should be of sustainably sourced timber, preferably treated with a non-toxic timber preservative. The posts should be the same length as the required height of the bed PLUS a minimum foundation depth of 30cm (12in). Foundation holes are dug to accommodate this buried part of the post, which can be held in place with rammed hardcore, ballast, or concrete.

The sides of the bed are best clad in boards or planks of timber, a minimum of 20mm (¾in) thick and 100mm (4in) wide, secured to posts at 600mm (2½in) spacings. Thicker timber holds its shape more readily and wider boards are quick to install, with the consequence that the support post can be at wider spacings. The most robust option would be to build the sides out of timber railway sleepers.

These vary in their dimensions but are commonly around 150mm (6in) thick, 250mm (10in) wide, and 2600mm (8ft 6in) in length. The weight of such sleepers will tend to hold them in position when secured to corner posts alone. If using untreated wood, you can add a timber preservative once the bed is constructed.

Equipment

Tape measure, bamboo canes, and string for marking out

Digging spade

Wood saw and protective gear (if cutting the timber yourself)

4 × square timber corner posts, 1000mm × 75mm × 75mm (3¼ft × 3in × 3in)

6 × side cladding timber planks, 1500mm × 150mm × 45mm (5ft × 6in × 1¾in)

6 × side cladding timber planks, 1000mm × 150mm × 45mm (3¼ft × 6in × 1¾in)

Medium-grit sandpaper (optional)

Electric drill with 6mm-gauge drill bit and countersink bit

48 × 6mm-gauge wood screws, 50mm (2in) long

Screwdriver

Spirit level

Soil, ballast, or concrete to fill foundation holes

> "For ease of construction and economy, building a retaining box structure out of timber is a great way to make a raised bed"

This simple bed can be scaled up to make larger sizes, and is suitable for ornamental and productive growing.

Basic construction

This simple rectangular structure consists of four corner posts, with side planks secured with screws.

Side planks can be attached to corner posts, prefabricating the short ends of the bed first.

1 metre (3¼ft)

1.5 metres (5ft)

Corner posts

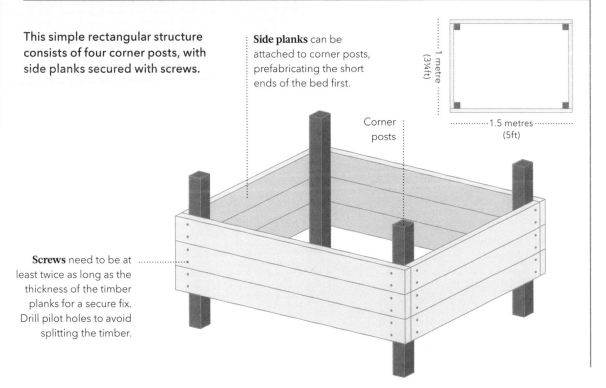

Screws need to be at least twice as long as the thickness of the timber planks for a secure fix. Drill pilot holes to avoid splitting the timber.

Instructions

Getting Started

Mark out the area of the raised-bed construction using bamboo canes and string. Check that the bed is the size you envisaged in your plans. Remember to allow for boards to overlap onto the support posts.

Dig out foundation pits for the corner posts to the depth of 30cm (12in), conserving the soil for use when filling the bed. Allow 10cm (4in) around each post to make a robust support.

1

Measure the required length of the planks for all the side walls – check your measurements at least twice to ensure you cut to the correct length.

2

Cut the planks with the wood saw, taking care to keep the saw blade at right angles to the timber. Alternatively, buy the planks pre-cut. Sand the edges with medium-grit sandpaper if necessary.

3

Drill pilot holes through the boards into the posts. Use a slightly thinner drill bit than the gauge of the coach screw shank. For a neat finish, you can use a countersink bit on the outside of each hole so that the head of the screw is flush with the timber.

01

02

04

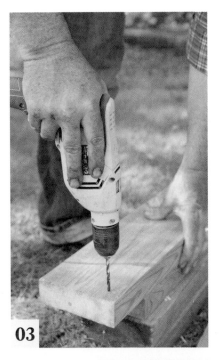

03

4
Screw one of the shorter side boards to a corner post, 20cm (8in) from the base. Make sure the board ends flush with the edge of the post to allow the side boards to overlap. Secure in place with two screws.

5
Attach another post to the other end of the board, then add the other two boards on this side to make it solid. Place the built short side in the foundation holes and use a spirit level to check that it will sit evenly. If necessary, dig away more earth in the foundation at the high end. Next, build the opposite end in the same way.

05

Instructions

6

Attach the longer boards to the corner posts, making sure each one overlaps the ends of the short side boards. Use two screws to attach the boards in place. Repeat for the other end.

7

Once the whole frame is constructed, set it in place with the bottom of each post located in holes in the ground at each corner. Check again that the top edge of the bed is level. If so, fill in the foundation holes with soil, ballast, or concrete around the base of each post.

8

To help preserve the timber for longer and retain moisture in the growing medium, line the sides of the bed with sheets of polythene. Fill the bed with an equal-parts mix of topsoil and organic-matter compost, topped off with 20cm (8in) of solely organic-matter compost (see pages 196–199) before planting up as desired.

06

08

07

Leaving the corner posts long at the top provides a useful prop to lean on when tending to plants, as well as a frame for protective netting or fleece.

Access matters

Keeping the corner posts long means you can increase the height of the raised bed where easy access is required, by adding extra side planks. Tailor the working height of the sides to suit individual requirements: as a guide, a finished height of 80–110cm (31–43in) is useful for standing access with limited mobility, while 60–70cm (24–28in) is recommended for wheelchair or seated access.

Metre-square bed

To get the most summer salads and crops in a small space, try making this simple square-metre bed to use on top of garden soil or an area of paving.

Ideal for new gardeners or those with limited space, metre-square growing is a great way to get bumper pickings. Where space allows, it is easy to make more of these raised beds by arranging them in a grid pattern with a 45-60cm (1½-2ft) path between them. Alternatively, scale up the length of the planks to make longer beds.

Subdividing the surface area of the beds is then easy using panel pins and twine. This will act as a guide when planting and sowing. Each small square could hold four young plants or a couple of short rows of seeds sown in shallow rows. See page 209 for details on sowing.

If you're installing your bed on top of uneven soil, excavate to a level base first before you begin. You can also add a timber preservative to the finished bed if using untreated wood.

Filled with a good-quality topsoil and topped off with some well-rotted organic matter, this compact growing space will prove highly productive. In such good conditions, you can grow plants close together, which will further save on the space needed for the tastes and succulence of summer.

Water the bed well once planted up and sown.

Construct this simple bed on a level area so the whole structure is square when screwed together. This will ensure that the growing surface is flat when filled.

Equipment

Tape measure, wood saw, and protective gear (if cutting the timber yourself)

4 × side cladding timber planks 1000mm × 150mm × 45mm (3¼ft × 6in × 1¾in)

Medium-grit sandpaper

4 × square timber corner posts 150mm × 50mm × 50mm (6in × 2in × 2in)

Electric drill with 6mm drill bit and countersink bit

16 × 6mm-gauge wood screws, 50mm (2in) long

Electric screwdriver

Topsoil mix

Organic-matter compost

Gritty horticultural sand

Panel pins, 25mm (1in), hammer, and garden twine

"Ideal for new gardeners or those with limited space, metre-square growing is a great way to get bumper pickings"

Sow seeds and plant seedlings of different plants in each of the bed's subdivisions.

Basic construction

These beds are structured as a simple square, 1 metre × 1 metre (3¼ft × 3¼ft) in size, secured with internal corner supports. The whole bed can be prefabricated before putting it in its final position.

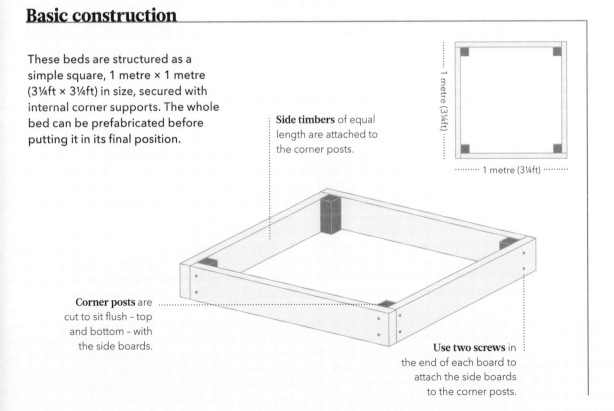

1 metre (3¼ft)

1 metre (3¼ft)

Side timbers of equal length are attached to the corner posts.

Corner posts are cut to sit flush – top and bottom – with the side boards.

Use two screws in the end of each board to attach the side boards to the corner posts.

Instructions

Getting started

Mark out and cut the timber cladding to the lengths specified on page 154 with a wood saw, taking care to keep the ends square and at right angles, or buy pre-cut. Use a medium-grit sandpaper to smooth the rough edges of the cuts.

1

Position the first corner post at the end of one of the timber sides, making sure it is flush with the end. Drill and countersink pilot holes approximately 2cm (¾in) up from the bottom and down from the top.

2

Screw the side to the corner post using the pilot holes. Drill, countersink, and screw the next side on the same corner post, taking care to overlap this board over the end of the first. Repeat the process for the rest of the corner posts and sides, making sure that each corner has one flush and one overlapping board, all in the same orientation so that the bed is square.

3

Line the base of the bed with a sheet of polythene or tarpaulin to prevent the topsoil mix washing out of the bottom. Fill the bed to within 3cm (1¼in) of the top with your chosen topsoil mix, taking care to firm it in place.

01 02

04

4
Top off with an organic-matter compost, mixed three parts by volume with one part gritty sand.

5
Mark a point halfway along each side and knock in a panel pin with a hammer, leaving 5mm (¼in) protruding to tie the horticultural twine in place.

6
Divide the remaining halves in two and mark with panel pins and twine. Then divide the bed surface into 16 small squares using the horticultural twine.

03

05 **06**

Explore Asian vegetables

Anja Klein

Raised beds have taken my vegetable gardening to a whole new level. When I took over my allotment garden 13 years ago, the soil was exhausted and compacted, a maple tree cast its shadow on the old vegetable beds, and, after some radical hedge pruning, I had a lot of twigs lying around. With a raised bed, I could solve all three problems at once.

A mix of Asian greens, such as tatsoi, mustard greens, and mizuna, can go straight from the veg bed to the kitchen.

Anja Klein, a gardener by passion, was born with a spade in her hand. She likes to drink expensive green tea and can't leave a garden market without buying something new. So that she can afford it all, she writes gardening books about raised beds, among other things.
www.der-kleine-horror-garten.de
Instagram: @derkleinehorrorgarten
Pinterest: @horrorgarten
YouTube: @kleinerhorrorgarten

Using raised beds in my allotment meant I could create better soil and move the plants closer to the light, and the hedge cuttings have simply disappeared into them.

My first raised bed was huge – it looked a bit like the black monolith from Stanley Kubrick's *2001: A Space Odyssey*. So it was no beauty, but the harvest from it was overwhelming. The black monolith accompanied me for 11 years. In the meantime, I have replaced it with more delicate raised beds made of building planks. There are more than 20 of them now – a bit crazy, but I just like growing vegetables in a clearly defined and delimited space. The garden is otherwise wild and colourful, so the raised beds are a nice contrast. They bring form and structure to the wilderness.

If you are planning a raised vegetable bed, why not choose particularly beautiful vegetables? After all, the eye eats with you. And in addition to beauty, you can also discover new tastes with unusual vegetables. Standard purple beetroot tastes too musty for you? Try a white or a bright orange variety. They taste much milder and fruitier. Or how about a carpaccio of pink-and-white striped beetroot? Chard already looks beautiful in the ordinary green variety, but how much more attractive are those with colourful stems? They shine more beautifully in the autumn sun than any flower.

My hop-in-the-wok raised bed

For this raised bed bursting with beautiful vegetables for an Asian-influenced kitchen, I have decided to use the square-foot (or square-metre) gardening method. When growing in squares, I simply get more types of vegetables in the bed. The squares are planted several times and I always harvest just enough to use directly in the kitchen.

My top piece of advice is to mix flowers with your vegetables. I like to plant tagetes or marigolds among mine. This has several advantages: they bring even more colour into the bed, the flowers are edible (*Tagetes tenuifolia* 'Tangerine Gem', for example, tastes refreshingly lemony), and their roots keep the soil healthy, as their excretions drive away harmful nematodes and wireworms.

A bed full of colourful veg, such as rainbow chard, is particularly appetizing.

PLANT LIST

For each seasonal bed, I divide the plot, which is 2 metres × 1 metre (6½ft × 3¼ft), into 18 squares of 33cm × 33cm (1ft × 1ft), each individually planted.

Spring

Asian greens
  (e.g. mustards,
  mizuna) × 16
Pak choi × 9
Radishes × 25
Tatsoi × 9
Chinese cabbage × 2
Asian lettuce × 16
Radishes × 16
Red kale × 1
Rainbow chard × 2
Red onions × 16
Oyster leaf / *Mertensia
  maritima* × 1
Rainbow chard × 2
Pumpkin × 1
Radishes × 25
Korean coriander /
  Oenanthe javanica × 1
Carrots × 25
Red onions × 16
Red kale × 1

Summer

new plantings:
Chinese cabbage × 2
Tagetes × 4
Thai basil / *Ocimum
  basilicum* var.
  thyrsiflora × 1
Marigolds /
  Calendula × 2
Spinach × 9
Tagetes × 4
Marigolds /
  Calendula × 2
Fennel × 4

Autumn

new plantings:
Spinach × 9
Spinach × 9

By autumn, the red onions are ready to harvest and their squares in the grid are taken by plantings of spinach.

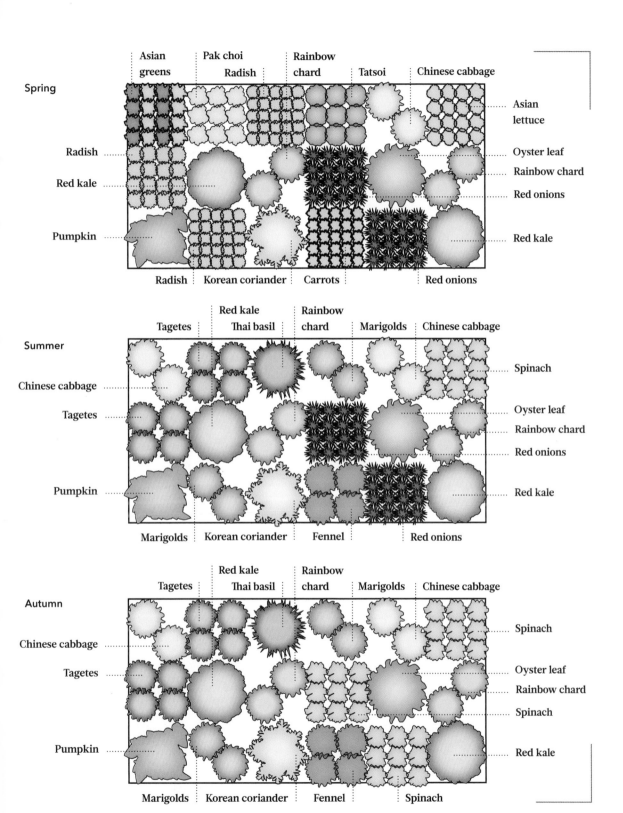

Spring

Asian greens
Pak choi
Radish
Rainbow chard
Tatsoi
Chinese cabbage
Asian lettuce
Radish
Oyster leaf
Red kale
Rainbow chard
Red onions
Pumpkin
Red kale
Radish
Korean coriander
Carrots
Red onions

Summer

Red kale
Thai basil
Rainbow chard
Tagetes
Marigolds
Chinese cabbage
Chinese cabbage
Spinach
Tagetes
Oyster leaf
Rainbow chard
Red onions
Pumpkin
Red kale
Marigolds
Korean coriander
Fennel
Red onions

Autumn

Red kale
Thai basil
Rainbow chard
Tagetes
Marigolds
Chinese cabbage
Chinese cabbage
Spinach
Tagetes
Oyster leaf
Rainbow chard
Spinach
Pumpkin
Red kale
Marigolds
Korean coriander
Fennel
Spinach

Herb tower

Making best use of the vertical space on a patio, balcony, or tiny courtyard, this layered mini raised bed is the perfect place to grow herbs close to where they can be used in the kitchen.

Composed of a series of progressively smaller beds, positioned at 45 degrees to each other, the growing space here is created in the corners of the beds while the centre acts as a storage reservoir for moisture, which the plants can root into.

Plant the base layer with herbs that like moisture, such as mint, and the top layer with those that prefer better drainage and aeration at their roots, like thyme. Watering the top of the pyramid will allow water to drain away from the upper levels and collect in the soil lower down.

This raised-bed design can be scaled up in size, and could incorporate more than the three layers shown here. Take care not to make it too large, or it won't be possible to lean in to tend or pick the herbs. If you're installing your tiered bed on top of uneven soil, excavate to a level base first before you begin. Once constructed, you can apply a stain and additional timber preservative if needed.

Simple to move around your garden or growing space, the beds are self-supporting when positioned on level ground but could be secured more firmly in place with long corner posts in each layer. This overall design with shallow layers could also be used to grow vegetables or alpine plants, or alternatively as an eye-catching focal point filled with spring or summer bedding plants.

Golden marjoram likes shade for part of the day (left); thyme grows well in drier conditions (right).

Equipment

Tape measure, wood saw, and protective gear (if cutting the timber planks yourself)

12 × square timber corner posts, 150mm × 50mm × 50mm (6in × 2in × 2in)

4 × side cladding timber planks, 650mm × 150mm × 45mm (2ft × 6in × 1¾in)

4 × side cladding timber planks, 420mm × 150mm × 45mm (1¼ft × 6in × 1¾in)

4 × side cladding timber planks, 250mm × 150mm × 45mm (10in × 6in × 1¾in)

Medium-grit sandpaper

Electric drill with 6mm drill bit and countersink bit

48 × 6mm-gauge wood screws, 50mm (2in) long

Electric screwdriver

Topsoil

Horticultural grit

> ## "Plant the base layer with herbs that like moisture, such as mint, and the top layer with those that prefer better drainage, like thyme"

A herb tower makes an attractive, productive addition to a patio or balcony.

Basic construction

This space-efficient planter consists of three square beds in decreasing sizes, stacked one on top of the other to create a tiered tower.

Position each bed at a 45-degree angle to the one below.

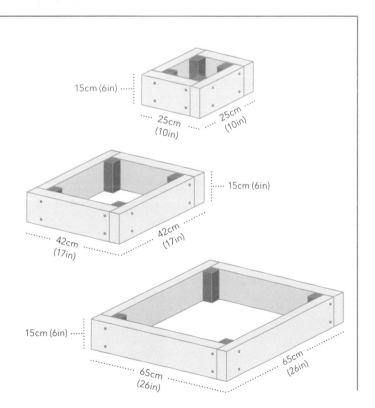

15cm (6in)

25cm (10in)

25cm (10in)

15cm (6in)

42cm (17in)

42cm (17in)

15cm (6in)

65cm (26in)

65cm (26in)

Instructions

1

Cut the planks and corner posts to length with a wood saw, or buy pre-cut, and use medium-grit sandpaper to remove splinters from the edges. Mock up each layer, with a post at each corner and overlapping one side plank over the end of the other.

2

Starting with the largest bed, pre-drill two pilot holes in the end of one side plank, making sure they are positioned to locate into the corner post.

3

Countersink the holes and screw the side plank to the corner post, taking care to make the corners square and tight.

4

Repeat the process described in steps 2 and 3 to attach both ends of each of the four planks to the four corner posts to make a square bed frame.

5

Repeat the assembly process for each of the smaller sized beds.

6

Assemble the layers, one on top of the other, the largest at the bottom. Position the corners of the upper layers in the middle of side plank of the bed beneath. Fill with a three parts topsoil, one part horticultural grit mix, which will be ideal for the herbs.

01

02

04

03

05

06

Malleable and mouldable metal

An adaptable building material, metal is available in various types to use for raised beds, and usually takes the form of steel or an alloy (a mix of different metals). Due to its inherent strength, metal can be used to make very thin supporting walls, which optimizes the space for growing.

Suitability

Ordinary steel is prone to rusting (oxidation in air) and needs some form of coating to stop this. Galvanized steel has a thin layer of non-reactive zinc applied to the surface, but other options include plastic or paint. Meanwhile, stainless steel involves adding chromium and other alloying metals during manufacture to create a rust-resistant material.

By contrast, COR-TEN Steel™, also known as weathering steel, is an alloy produced by the addition of phosphorus, chromium, nickel, and copper. This gives it great strength but allows the surface to rust, forming a decorative, protective coat.

Other useful constructional metals include aluminium alloys (with small quantities of another metal added), which, though not prone to rusting, do corrode or oxidize to produce an aluminium oxide protective coating to the outer surface. These alloys are strong but lightweight. Metal can also be corrugated to add end-to-end strength (along the lines of the corrugation), allowing thinner material to be used than when in sheet form.

The disadvantage of using metals for raised beds is that they transmit heat and cold very readily, into the soil and root area immediately inside. This can cause stress to the roots of plants, as well as the crucially beneficial soil organisms.

In many cases, basic (the cheapest) metals will work out to be more expensive than timber but usually cost less than brick or stone to build with. As they can be bent and formed, metals also offer the option for bespoke designs.

Tips for building with metal

Sheets of metal offer a strong and lightweight means of construction and are relatively quick to build with. They are far from self-supporting, however. All types of sheet metal are available in different thicknesses, but the thicker the gauge, the more expensive it will be.

Metal can be easily bent to make curving shapes and circles.

COR-TEN steel can be used to make water features and matching raised beds.

Corner and intermediate posts, as well as horizontal internal bracings, will be necessary to form a strong framework to prevent the metal from bending or flexing. Such supports can be made of box-section metal or timber and their spacing will depend on the thickness of the sheet metal used. On average, vertical supports should be spaced 30–40cm (12–16in) apart with horizontal bracings 30cm (12in) apart.

Where the metal beds exceed 30cm (12in) in height, it will be necessary to concrete the upright supports into the ground. Allow a foundation depth of half the height of the bed for corner and intermediate support posts and secure them in place using the concrete mix specified on page 177.

Internal bracings from one side of the bed to the other are also needed to prevent the weight of the soil from pushing out the sides. Position these at the bottom and just below the top of the bed at 30–40cm (12–16in) spacings. Drill and bolt (metal) or screw (timber) the framework together before attaching corrugated or sheet metal to the outside. Secure in place with bolts or screws at 10–15cm (4–6in) spacings.

Off-the-shelf metal raised-bed kits (see page 168) offer a quick and easy method of construction but are rarely made from thick-gauge metal. Bespoke beds and planters offer a robust and long-life option, though these are generally expensive.

Maintenance

Metals used in construction may be liable to rusting or other forms of corrosion. Painting with an appropriate formulation for the particular metal and situation will extend life and maintain an attractive finish. Corrugated and sheet metals are usually available in a zinc-coated or plastic paint finish, which will protect them. Always use these to paint any freshly cut edges to prevent rust getting a foothold. Other metals, such as stainless and COR-TEN steels, provide their own rust protection – in the case of the latter, with rust itself!

Sharp edges

The thin top edge of sheet metals can be sharp to the touch and cause cuts. In some cases, the edges are rolled over to protect against this, but corners can still be dangerous. Good ways to cover these include attaching a timber strip on each side along the top to overlap the edge or splitting a length of plastic hosepipe to feed over and cover the edge.

Child's metal keyhole bed

Corrugated metal kits can be configured in different permutations as they come in sections that bolt together. This example, with rounded ends and straight sides, could be adapted into a keyhole bed.

A keyhole bed is a fun, quirky design, ideal for budding young gardeners. This metal raised bed is designed to be constructed on top of soil. Digging into the ground to a depth of around 10cm (4in) will help retain the base of the finished bed and allows it to be adjusted for level if the site is sloping. Using a prefabricated kit, which comprises both curved and straight corrugated sections, means that it comes with all the nuts and bolts included to connect the panels together.

Adapting the kit into a keyhole bed simply involves using square timber corner posts, and attaching the metal to them using wood screws through the pre-drilled bolt holes in the corrugated panels. Long pegs of the same timber, which are knocked into the ground once the bed is in place, give extra strength and support to the sides of the finished construction.

A large, recycled plastic tree pot with the bottom cut out is positioned at the centre of this bed to act as a homemade composting bucket. This can be lifted up as the compost decomposes and the nutritious material scraped back onto the soil in the surrounding bed.

Equipment

Corrugated metal raised-bed kit or similar: 1500mm (5ft) diameter, 360mm (1¼ft) high. Made of pre-formed, curved, and straight panel sections. Nuts and bolts come with the kit

Spanner and socket set to tighten nuts and bolts

Wood saw (if cutting the timber yourself)

4 × square timber corner posts, 360mm × 50mm × 50mm (1¼ft × 2in × 2in)

24 × 6mm-gauge wood screws, 25mm (1in) long

Electric screwdriver

Sledgehammer to knock in support pegs

8 × timber support pegs, 500mm × 50mm × 50mm (1½ft × 2in × 2in), with a point at one end

30-litre (6½-gallon) plastic tree pot (recycled if possible)

Topsoil

Basic construction

The wedge-shaped access point and central compost bin of this curved bed resemble a keyhole.

Four square timber posts give corner support to the basic structure of the bed.

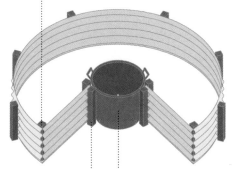

Eight timber support pegs around the sides provide extra stability.

A large black recycled plastic plant pot in the centre acts as a composting bin.

"A keyhole bed is a fun, quirky design, ideal for budding young gardeners"

Instructions

1

Lay out the curved sections of
the raised-bed kit. Keep back
two of the sections that make
a complete circle.

2

Bolt the curved pieces together
to make a circle with a segment
missing. Cut the post timber to
length with a wood saw (or buy
pre-cut), the same as the depth
of the bed. Screw one piece of
this timber to each end of the
incomplete corrugated metal
circle, through the bolt holes.

3

Screw the end of one of the
straight corrugated pieces to
each of the corner posts, facing
inwards at right angles to the
edge of the circle. Screw a corner
post timber to the other end of
each of the straight sections. Use
one of the spare curved sections
to join the inside ends of the
straight sections, in the same
orientation as the outside curve.

The pot at the centre
of the bed is a compost bin
where green waste can
be left to wilt and begin
decomposing before being
added to the bed.

01

02

03

04

05

06

4
Set the bed in position. Measure across the circumference to check the circle is round. With the sledgehammer, knock the timber support pegs into the ground at regular intervals around the outside edge of the corrugated panels.

5
Set the large plastic pot at the centre of the circle ready to fill with composting raw materials. Fill the bed with an appropriate topsoil mix.

6
Help the child to plant the bed with bright, easy-to-grow, fun plants such as rudbeckias, sunflowers, celosia, and sweetcorn. Ideas for decoration could include a scarecrow, wind spinners, ceramic toadstools, and a gravel mulch area for playing with toys.

Plant kid-friendly beds

Thomas Berolzheimer

My six raised beds are the heart of my garden, catching the best sunlight. While the rest of my yard is full of perennials, foundational shrubs, trees, and grasses, I use my raised beds for continuous displays and harvests of annual veg and flowers. These beds not only nurture the plants, but also cultivate curiosity, patience, and love for nature in children.

The bright, cheerful colours of zinnias will encourage children to get growing and engage with nature.

Thomas Berolzheimer is a photographer and entrepreneur with a dedication to gardening, who has cultivated his passion for plants over the past seven years. He recently launched Nimble Garden Company, an initiative focused on educating and inspiring gardeners.

Thomas's collaborative work alongside his wife can be seen on Instagram at @juliaberolzheimer, while his gardening insights are shared on @nimblegardenco.

I plant my raised beds in waves, ensuring something is always in full swing. Their yield exploded when I switched to "no-dig" in 2020. The top 15cm (6in) of soil are pure compost, and the rest is a half-and-half mix of compost and topsoil. This maintains the beds' volume, and with each new planting, I simply add more compost on top. The beds, featuring mostly flowers this year, buzz with bees, bringing vibrant life to the garden.

Designed on a gentle slope, 30–45cm (12–18in) tall, the beds' set-up deters trampling while also granting easy access for tiny hands to dig, plant, and harvest. My children adore them.

In fact, these delightful garden beds are a treasure trove of experiences for kids. They can watch as their green beans, lettuce, and cucumbers sprout and grow, then revel in the excitement of harvesting their very own produce. The beds act as a buffet, encouraging them to taste fresh vegetables. Root crops introduce them to the hidden world beneath the soil surface, while tending to their strawberry plants teaches them about the plant's life cycle from flower to ripe fruit. They enjoy deadheading and preparing floral bouquets, too.

Raised beds are also a conversation piece, encouraging exchanges with neighbours and passers-by. The joy these beds bring to my family and the local wildlife is immeasurable.

PLANT LIST

Bed 1

This compact bed, 90cm × 2.5 metres (3ft × 8ft), is a sweet treat for young gardeners, with strawberry plants interspersed with sweet alyssum for an added olfactory delight that attracts beneficial insects.

Strawberries × 5
Sweet alyssum / *Lobularia maritima* × 5

Bed 2

This spacious plot, 45cm × 1.4 metres (1½ft × 4½ft), combines colourful zinnias and marigolds with an array of tasty, easy-to-grow edibles.

Dwarf zinnias × 6
Marigolds / *Calendula* × 8
Dwarf bush green beans × 4
Hearting lettuce × 3
Scallions (green onions)
Basil × 3
Dwarf tomato (with trellis) × 1
Dwarf peas (with trellis) × 1
Dwarf bush cucumber
   (with trellis) × 1
Carrots × 14
Potatoes × 4
Radishes × 5

Bed 1

Strawberries ......
Sweet alyssum

Sweet alyssum ......
Strawberries

Strawberries ......
Sweet alyssum

Sweet alyssum ......
Strawberries

Strawberries ......

Sweet alyssum

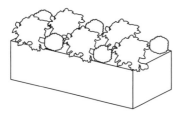

A bed of sweet strawberries and scented sweet alyssum provides a sensory gardening experience for children.

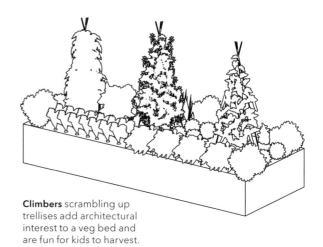

Climbers scrambling up trellises add architectural interest to a veg bed and are fun for kids to harvest.

Bed 2

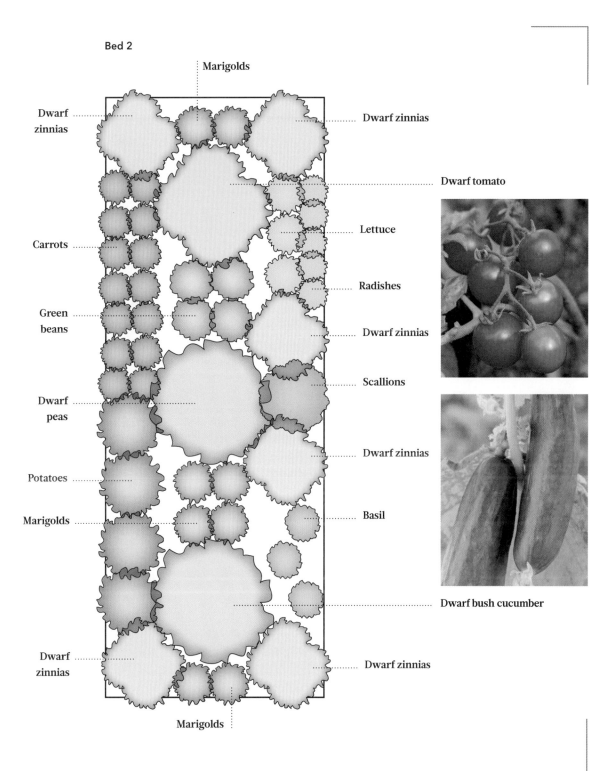

Marigolds

Dwarf zinnias

Dwarf zinnias

Dwarf tomato

Carrots

Lettuce

Green beans

Radishes

Dwarf zinnias

Dwarf peas

Scallions

Dwarf zinnias

Potatoes

Marigolds

Basil

Dwarf bush cucumber

Dwarf zinnias

Dwarf zinnias

Marigolds

175

Building blocks of permanence

Bricks and dense concrete blocks offer a robust and durable material for the construction of raised beds. Each unit has its own density and weight, while the standardized, rectangular shape gives them stability. Bonded together in layers or "courses" using cement mortar, they can be used to build solid supporting walls to contain soil.

Suitability

Made from clay, with additions of sand and ash, kiln-fired bricks are weather resistant and long lasting. They can also be reclaimed and reused. Their small unit size allows them to be built into both geometric and simple free-form shapes, and a wide range of different brick colours allows for a variety of effects.

Meanwhile, larger dense concrete blocks are made, as the name suggests, from aerated concrete poured into moulds. Their large size means that they are less adaptable to curves, but they can be used in conjunction with bricks for complex shapes. Brick walls are characterful, but blockwork walls may be rendered or painted to make them less utilitarian in appearance.

Using these materials allows raised-bed walls to be successfully incorporated into steps and retaining walls for a fully integrated look. Once built, these beds are pretty permanent and difficult to reconfigure.

Both of these dense building materials have the capacity to absorb radiant heat energy from the sun, without conducting too much into the soil behind them. And while individual bricks are fairly lightweight to work with, blocks are heavy and can be tricky to install for the amateur. In addition, building decent walls requires a high level of skill and time, and may require a professional builder, adding considerably to the cost of the project.

Bricks and blocks can be stacked, without mortar, to make low-level raised beds.

Mortar-built brick walls provide long-lasting support for permanent beds. Here, the soil level has been left lower to allow seedling crops to be covered early in the season.

Concrete for foundations

Good foundations are essential for brick, block, and mortared stone walls. Make a strong concrete mix using the following parts by volume:

Mix the dry ingredients thoroughly, before slowly adding small volumes of water and mixing all the while to make a stiff concrete that holds its shape without slumping or flowing.

1 part ordinary Portland cement

3 parts sharp sand

6 parts aggregate

Tips for building with brick and blockwork

For a simple edge to retain the soil in a very shallow raised bed, bricks or concrete blocks can simply be laid flat, end to end, without mortar but not exceeding 15cm (6in) high. Any taller and the weight of the topsoil inside the bed will quickly displace them.

For taller walls, therefore, unless building on a pre-existing concrete pad or solid paved area, it will be necessary to install a strip foundation in the ground prior to building. This consists of digging out a trench in the soil, a minimum of 35cm (14in) deep and 20cm (8in) wide, to remove the topsoil, which could otherwise settle unevenly under the weight of the wall, causing cracks to appear.

Fill the bottom of the trench with a minimum of 15cm (6in) concrete (see page 177) for walls up to 40cm (16in) high – make this foundation deeper for

taller walls. The concrete is best allowed to set and "cure" for at least four days before starting to build the retaining walls on it.

A sand and cement mortar mix is used to bond the individual bricks or blocks together to form a wall (see opposite). As far as tips go, avoid laying bricks or blocks in hot, dry weather or in cold, frosty conditions, as this can affect the mortar. It is also a good idea to wet the bricks or blocks and then stand them to drain before laying them, as a damp surface will provide good adhesion with the mortar.

Building with bricks

The dimensions of household bricks vary, but in the UK they are generally around 215mm (8½in) long by 102.5mm (4in) wide and 65mm (2½in) deep. They usually have some form of hollow or "frog" in the top or three holes that run through from top to bottom. This is to increase the surface area that comes into contact with the mortar to create a stronger bond. The frog is usually laid facing upwards, until the last layer (course) of brick is

Creative designs are easy to build with standard house bricks.

Timber planks make a stylish contrasting top or coping for brick and block beds.

installed, when the frog faces down to prevent water collecting in the top of the wall.

For maximum strength, the joints in brick (and block) walls should be positioned so that the brick in the next layer spans the join of the bricks below. This creates a pattern in the finished wall called the "bond", and the simplest form of this is known as the "stretcher" or "running" bond.

For a single thickness of wall, the bricks are laid end to end along their length, on a 1cm (½in) deep bed of mortar. A double-thickness wall uses pairs of bricks laid in parallel with 1cm (½in) of mortar between them. In this case, the next course of bricks can be set at right angles so that each brick spans across the width of the previous layer. Alternating layers can be built up in this way.

It pays to use a line and spirit level to keep the wall even and "plumb" (vertical), and to clean up excess mortar to try to keep the bricks clean. Once the mortar has hardened after a couple of days, the gaps between the bricks can be filled or "pointed" with mortar to provide extra strength and to create a neat finish.

Blockwork for speed

A good alternative to bricks, dense concrete blocks are quicker to build with, though much heavier to handle. This can make them harder to keep level and plumb.

Blocks can be laid on their edge along their length to create a single-block thickness, or flat along their length for a wider, stronger wall. The width of mortar is usually the same as that used for bricks. The rough surface of the blocks helps them to bond together.

Maintenance

Brick and block walls are relatively care-free but may require occasional cleaning and repointing to keep them in the best condition.

Mortar mix for bricks

A good all-purpose mix for brick and blockwork mortar contains the following:

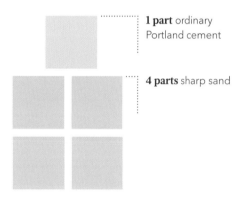

1 part ordinary Portland cement

4 parts sharp sand

For pointing (filling any spaces between the bricks or blocks once the wall has been built and is set) make the mix using:

1 part ordinary Portland cement

3 parts sharp sand

In both cases, mix the ingredients dry, then add a little water at a time while mixing, to form a stiff paste that holds its shape well.

Tough and traditional stone

With a variety of colours and types, both natural and reconstituted stone offer a wide range of ornamental materials.

Suitability

Rough natural stone comes in its quarried form, so is available in a large selection of shapes and sizes, although it can be graded to make building easier. This is a good material to use when creating free-form raised-bed shapes. It can be used to create a dry-stone wall – something that requires considerable skill if it is to be more than a couple of rock layers high – or held in position with a cement mortar (see page 179), which is easier.

Un-mortared or dry-stone walls are built using the natural layers in the stone as a guide.

By contrast, "dressed" stone is formed, either by hand or machine, to make more regularly shaped blocks to work with. These are the more expensive option and will often vary in size, but the square or rectangular forms give straight edges to work with.

Taking a similar form, reconstituted stone and stone-faced blocks provide an often cheaper alternative to dressed, natural stone. Both are best installed with a narrow band of mortar so as not to detract from the stone itself.

As with brick and blockwork, the results are robust and durable, but also permanent and difficult to reconfigure without demolition. And not only is stone heavy and often rough to work with, it is also expensive and usually requires skilled builders to install it.

Tips for building with stone

Edgings to shallow beds and more substantial walls for raised beds can be made from a range of different types of natural rock. Sandstone, limestone, gritstone, and granite are probably the most widely available and easiest to use in raised-bed construction.

Whether you're building a dry-stone (un-mortared) or mortared wall, choose pieces with a broadly flat, square, cornered shape. Rounded flint and boulders are challenging to use.

As with brick and block constructions, a stone wall more than around 20cm (8in) high will require foundations to maintain its stability. For dry-stone walls this can take the form of a 35cm (14in) deep trench, 20cm (8in) wide, filled with crushed stone or ballast and rammed into place. For mortared walls, it is best to use a concrete foundation (see page 177).

Meanwhile, the more uniform dressed stone can be built up in a similar way to brick and blockwork with a regular mortar layer.

The most refined stone surface finishes are applied in the form of slabs or tiles. They are attached with adhesive or mortared in place, onto a blockwork or pre-cast concrete structure.

Maintenance

Stone walls may require occasional cleaning and repointing to keep them in the best condition, but otherwise they require very little maintenance.

Chunky blocks are quicker to build with than random stone.

Build with a framework

When building a rough-hewn stone wall using mortar, it may be useful to build a wooden framework or "former". This involves using timber and sheets of plyboard to create a flat surface, against which the outer face of the wall can be built. The structure will help to keep the stones even and flush with each other, holding them in place while the mortar sets. The former is then removed and can be reused to build subsequent walls to form a raised bed.

Moulded to fit

When it comes to more bespoke designs for raised beds, there are a couple of moulded options that may be considered. These may be required for unique shapes and forms, or where a long-term permanent structure is required.

Suitability

As discussed earlier, metals can be bent, forged, or cast into different shapes, but this is usually done off-site, prior to installation, and requires careful measurement and planning.

For in-situ constructions, glass-reinforced plastic (see opposite) can be moulded on-site, but for best results and finish this is usually done by specialist companies. It is a good way of getting a waterproof bed if that is required for a pond or rooftop installation, but make sure the latter has provision for appropriate drainage to prevent soil from becoming saturated. Key benefits are that it is low maintenance and has good insulation properties, but this is one of the most expensive options.

Poured concrete is another alternative, and while large and complex projects are best installed professionally, smaller raised beds can be made by someone with good DIY skills. The resulting concrete has similar thermal properties to bricks and blocks, and can be left raw or painted. It can also be disguised by building a brick, timber, or metal skin around the outside. Adequate provision is needed for drainage, if the bed is to be planted, but this type of construction can also be made watertight using a sealant to create a raised pond.

Tips for building with concrete

Shuttered concrete is a useful option for a raised bed, particularly when a seamless finish or additional structural integrity is required.

The process involves building a temporary mould for the wet concrete to be poured into. A timber framework, known as a formwork or shutter, is used to create an outer and inner skin to hold the concrete in place while it sets.

The walls would need to be at least 15cm (6in) thick, with added strength provided by incorporating metal reinforcement bar ("rebar") panels into the mould and wiring them together at the corners. For easy removal of the formwork mould, the internal surface of the plywood can be treated with mould-release oil or lined with thick polythene sheeting.

Concrete should be left for at least four days to set and begin the "curing" process by which it attains full strength. The mould can then be removed, and the walls left for a further 10 days before filling with topsoil mix or installing a waterproof lining to create a pond.

Maintenance

For metal see page 167; for plastics see page 184. Aside from basic cleaning and the upkeep of any paintwork, concrete is very easy to maintain.

Rounded blockwork corners can be rendered to create a smooth curve.

Complex curves can be accommodated by casting concrete supporting walls in-situ (top). Smooth, rendered finishes can be painted with masonry paint in your choice of colour (above).

Moulded plastic

Glass-reinforced plastic (GRP) can offer another form of bespoke raised bed, but in most cases it is beyond the abilities of the home DIY-er. A formwork is usually built using timber and plywood to create the shape in which the GRP is installed using alternate layers of fibreglass and catalysed resin. This needs to be built up to a sufficient thickness to withstand the weight of soil that will be contained in the bed, which usually means that it is very costly. It can be suitable to waterproof the inside of a concrete, block, or brickwork raised bed on a balcony or roof, where the strength is provided by the other materials. All surfaces need to be clean and dry for the installation, which means that specialist contractors are best used, who will also have relevant protective clothing.

Plastics and composite materials

Manufactured materials can also be used to build walls for raised beds – uPVC or composite materials, such as glass-reinforced plastic (GRP), are produced in dense panel and board formats. These can be used as a rot-proof alternative to timber, though generally at a slightly higher price.

Suitability

Some types of plastic are prone to degradation by sunlight, which makes them brittle, but ultra-violet (UV) light-stabilized uPVC is much more durable and long lasting, the main advantage being that it requires little or no maintenance. Where facilities are available, a limited range of plastic materials can be recycled, which may lessen concerns over their use and the possibility of them ending up in landfill, but it is worth checking when buying.

Plastic boards are usually available in a small range of colours, but these tend to be more expensive than standard white. Overall, uPVC and composite materials have moderate insulation properties, which means they do not conduct too much heat or cold from the outside air into the soil and roots in the bed. However, remember that white and pale colours will reflect light and radiant energy from the sun, while black and dark colours will absorb it and pass more heat into the soil.

Tips for building with plastics and composites

Ready-made plastic panels can be used as a substitute for timber, but make sure they are supported by a robust frame, particularly if thin sheets are used. Alternatively, use the panels to clad the outside of timber or metal structures.

Constructions made of glass-reinforced plastic are best undertaken by specialist installers, which, as a result, makes them an expensive option.

Maintenance

Plastics and GRP are generally maintenance free, although exposure to sunlight and extremes of temperature will ultimately cause them to degrade.

These thick, rigid plastic beds are given extra support by a metal frame for a stylish look.

Thinking outside the box

There are a whole host of other ways to make walls for raised beds, or to form large containers for soil – many of them extremely cost effective and environmentally friendly – from gabions to industrial containers to a recycled domestic bathtub.

Rock-filled gabion cages make ideal support walls for terraced and raised beds.

Suitability

Metal cage gabions, filled with stone, rocks, cobbles, rubble, recycled bottles, or other materials, are a good option for building raised beds as the look they give can suit both rural and urban locations, as well as informal and formal installations. They create broad, stable walls, with the added benefit that a range of wildlife habitats are created in the open spaces between each piece of fill material.

When it comes to recycled materials, there is plenty that can be pressed into service for another use so that we lessen our impact on the planet by creating new materials and reducing the amount of old stuff that goes into landfill. Tyres have a long life and great insulation properties. The latter reduces cold penetration in winter, but their black colour means they also absorb heat from the sun and thus warm the soil they contain. This can be useful for encouraging early growth of crops as well as flowering plants.

Straw bales also have good insulation properties, but their life is limited to just a few years as they will decompose. Initially, however, they will perform the useful function of retaining soil in a bed and help to improve the soil as the straw is slowly broken down into valuable organic matter by microorganisms.

As for impromptu containers, it doesn't need much imagination to turn woven polypropylene bulk bags (used for soil and building materials) into a raised bed. Many of them have a volume of around a cubic metre, which will provide a good depth of soil to help keep the root run cool and moist. The tough material is very resistant, so although it will bulge around the sides due to the weight of the material it is filled with, it won't rip.

Other product containers can be used, in particular industrial-grade intermediate bulk containers (IBC), which consist of a high-density polyethylene tank, supported in a galvanized metal cage. With the top cut out and some drainage holes punched in the base, the tank can be filled with a soil-and-compost mix. And while there are plenty of domestic containers that can find a second use as planters, baths and loft tanks are particularly useful, as they are large enough to hold a good volume of soil for crops or ornamentals.

Tips for building with gabions

Gabions can be square or rectangular in shape and are available in a wide range of different sizes with a lid of the same construction that is wired in place once filled. For raised beds, it is important to consider the width of the basket and how much space it will take up overall, compared to the size of the cultivable area. In most cases, gabions will only need to be one or two baskets high to form raised-bed walls.

When building on soil, it is essential to dig out the topsoil where the baskets are to be seated, to a depth of at least 35cm (14in). This will help to secure them in position. Install the basket empty and wire them together for extra stability. A liner cut from a close-weave geotextile can then be installed in the sides and base of each gabion if they are to be filled with soil, gravel, or crushed stone.

Where big pieces of rock or other large fill materials are used, it is worth taking time to stack them carefully inside the visible face so it looks even and to maximize stability. The inner part of the gabion can be filled more randomly. Once filled, line the inner face of the gabion wall with a geotextile to prevent topsoil washing away into the fill material.

Fillings for gabions

The size of the fill material will depend on the mesh gauge of the gabion. The cage can be lined with a geotextile to retain finer fill materials. Here are the most common options:

- Rough-hewn rock
- Boulders and cobbles
- Broken salvaged brick
- Stacked glass bottles
- Logs
- Old lawn turf and soil
- Geotextile with gravel or crushed stone

Tips for building with recycled materials

The most obvious recycled materials to use for raised beds are bricks to build walls, or second-hand scaffold boards, timber, and old pallets. And there are lots of sheet metals that can be reused, too. Take care to remove any old nails, screws, and fixings first before construction to prevent injury or damage to tools.

Of the sundry other things available, bulk bags and storage containers are easiest and quickest to use for raised beds. Bulk bags come in many sizes depending on their original purpose, but the most useful are those in which building materials are delivered. Meanwhile, if using plastic intermediate bulk containers (IBCs) and rigid plastic pallet boxes as instant containers, remember to make lots of drainage holes in the base and lower corners, and fill the bottom of them with a 7.5cm (3in) layer of

Cobbles form the filling between a sandwich of wire mesh to create an attractive retaining wall.

Improvised beds are quick and easy to make using transport crates and vintage containers like this recycled water tank.

drainage material, such as crushed stone or expanded clay pebbles (see page 196).

For an industrial look, old waste skips can sometimes be picked up cheaply and are sufficiently robust to hold soil without reinforcement. Large drainage holes in the base and sides are essential, together with at least 10cm (4in) of crushed stone in the bottom. Cover this with a sheet of geotextile to prevent the soil washing into this layer and impeding drainage.

Second-hand domestic baths can be obtained for next to nothing and come with a drainage hole already installed! Their sides can be supported and disguised with a timber framework and cladding where they need to look smart. Even old wardrobes and chests of drawers can be flipped onto their back and filled with topsoil. And for the fun-loving grower, why not finish off a standard raised bed with an ornate metal bed frame or headboard?

Tips for building with tyres

Easily stacked in place, old tyres are a quick way to make a retaining wall to contain a raised bed. It is worth trying to source tyres of a similar size and scrubbing them clean of excess dirt.

Their inherent weight means that a single layer of tyres can simply be laid flat, directly on the ground

or a solid surface to retain a shallow bed of topsoil. However, where more than one layer is used, holes should be drilled in the tread and walls of the tyres to connect them together, using either thick-gauge wire or bolts. This will provide stability to the structure. It is not advisable to exceed three layers of tyres in height, however, as the weight of the soil in the bed may push them over.

Fill the inside of the tyres with packed earth as the wall is built up. This will help to hold them in place and provide extra growing space in the finished bed. Alternatively, the top of the tyre walls can be finished off with a coping of timber planks to prevent dirt from the tyres rubbing onto clothing.

Instant raised beds

Tractor and lorry tyres can be used individually to make raised beds. Lay the tyre flat on a solid surface or dig out topsoil to around 30cm (12in) when installing on open earth. With the tyre in place, put a 10cm (4in) layer of crushed stone in the base before using any excavated soil as a basis for the topsoil fill.

The tops of straw bales can be excavated and filled with topsoil for planting (left). Add leaky hose irrigation and straw mulch to the surface after planting to maintain moisture in the bale (right).

Tips for building with straw bales

Raised-bed walls can be built from square straw bales as a temporary measure, either when they are only needed for a couple of seasons or when rapid soil improvement is required. It is particularly useful as a system for growing vegetables and cut flowers.

The bed only needs to be one bale deep and is best made by laying them on their side, with the ends of the straws pointing up from the top of the bale. This will ensure that the sides of the straws, which are more waterproof, will be in contact with the soil filling and thus less likely to rot away quickly.

The straw will eventually decompose in contact with the soil and moisture, generally on the inner side of the wall, but it will usually take two to three seasons to fully rot down. This will provide lots of organic matter, which can be mixed into the growing medium used to originally fill the bed. Subsequently, this mix can be used to fill another straw-bale bed, or a more permanent structure. The technique is an adapted form of "straw-bale growing", in which planting pockets are cut into the top of a bale, filled with a little soil or compost, and then planted with quick-to-mature summer vegetable plants. By using straw bales in this way to make the retaining wall for a raised bed, the growing area is optimized even more effectively.

Lining raised beds

The type of construction used to make a raised bed will dictate whether it needs to be lined, and what type of lining material to use. In most cases this simply involves lining the inside of the walls rather than the base.

Timber structures can be lined with polythene to help reduce moisture coming into contact with the wood, which will cause it to rot. This is especially important as the inner surface can't be re-treated with timber preservative unless the bed is emptied, so the polythene reduces the need for this. The lining has the added benefit of stopping soil washing out through narrow gaps between the wooden planks – an important consideration where less uniform, recycled timber is used.

Such topsoil seepage is less of a problem where metal is used for construction – although corrugated sheets can create weep holes. More important is to line with a material that will help to insulate the soil, and thus the plant roots, from the sun's heat transmitted through the metal (see page 166), in particular on the south-facing side of the bed. A couple of layers of sacking, bubble polythene, or even sheets of fibreboard or ply will keep the soil cool and moist, as well as helping to insulate it from the winter cold.

Solid brick, blockwork, and stone walls can be left unlined, unless the bed is to be used as a raised pond or bog garden. In this case – as with all other types of construction – a PVC or butyl liner would be needed to retain the water. This lining would need to be punctured in a few places for a bog garden, however, to prevent the soil from becoming totally waterlogged.

Both permanent raised beds built from gabion baskets and temporary ones using straw can be usefully lined on the inside of the walls with a woven landscape fabric or polythene. This will prevent the soil from washing out.

Thick polythene creates a moisture barrier where soil comes into contact with the inside of a timber raised bed.

Filling a bed: importance of soil

To get the best from raised-bed growing it pays to understand about soil and the intimate relationship that it has with the roots of plants. Nature has perfected this interface over millions of years, and learning from this gives the gardener the knowledge and skill to manipulate the growing environment for the best results.

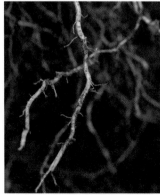

The fine, thread-like hairs on plant roots protrude between soil particles to allow them to extract moisture.

Healthy soil is not just an inert, lifeless material. It is teeming with life and has a whole array of functions for the plants that grow in it. Because soil is under our feet, it has been rather "out of sight, out of mind" in the past, to the point where it has been said that we know more about the observable, near side of the moon than we know about soil. And the fact that we sometimes refer to it as "dirt" shows just how much it has been disregarded.

To this end, it is also easy to think that we have to fill raised beds with decent garden compost to get good results. But as we will see, compost is in fact only part of the story. A good natural soil is the best growing medium, enabling plants to grow more robustly and cope with environmental extremes – something that is more important than ever when faced with a changing climate.

Soils have been formed by the weathering of rocks at the earth's surface, together with the decomposition of dead plant and animal remains. The whole production is orchestrated and mixed by a complex web of life, providing a means by which chemical elements – most notably carbon, nitrogen, and oxygen – are recycled into compounds and back to their elemental state.

The easiest way to understand soil is to think of it in terms of the two inputs: the mineral matter from the bottom, and the organic matter from the top. The "Goldilocks" zone where these two inputs are well mixed is referred to as the topsoil, beneath which is subsoil, which contains progressively less organic matter and proportionately more mineral matter derived from different types of underlying rocks. The different chemicals that the rocks contain determine the types of nutrients in the resultant soil and its relative acidity or alkalinity (pH level), something which profoundly affects the types of plants that can grow in it (see page 192).

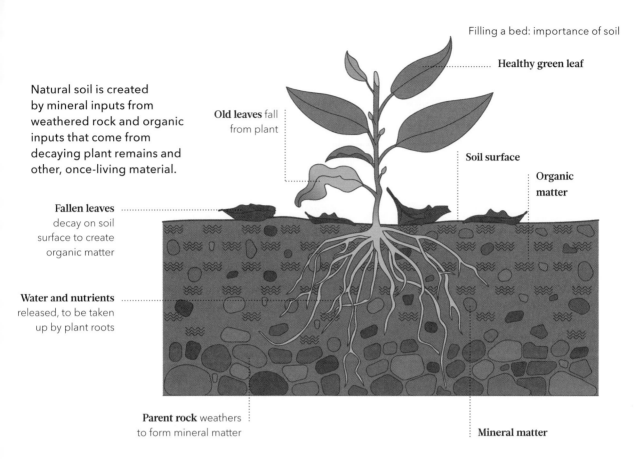

Healthy green leaf

Natural soil is created by mineral inputs from weathered rock and organic inputs that come from decaying plant remains and other, once-living material.

Old leaves fall from plant

Soil surface

Organic matter

Fallen leaves decay on soil surface to create organic matter

Water and nutrients released, to be taken up by plant roots

Parent rock weathers to form mineral matter

Mineral matter

Soil: the ideal growing medium

The majority of the plants we cultivate have evolved to take advantage of the soil in which they grow. The relationship between plant roots and the soil is crucial and depends on a moisture-retentive yet well-aerated structure.

Fundamentally, soil provides a growing medium into which roots can spread to support the upright top growth. In addition, the organic matter in the soil will act as a sponge to hold on to moisture and nutrients for the plants to use as required.

Meanwhile, the inorganic constituent of the soil – the mineral matter from the underlying rocks – will release nutrients, too. It also adds weight to the soil to increase stability for the plants, and helps to maintain an open, free-draining, aerated structure – which is necessary for healthy root development.

There are also huge benefits to be had from the biological connections with other soil organisms, which are best maintained by growing in soil, rather than pure compost.

What is meant by...?

Soil: A naturally occurring mix of inorganic (mineral) matter and organic (both living and dead) matter. It varies widely in its formation and characteristics.

Compost: The decomposed remains of organic matter; it is also used to refer to a mixture or "formulation" of different constituents used by gardeners as an alternative to natural soil. Compost may contain both inorganic and organic constituents. General purpose and highly specific composts can be tailored to suit particular plants and growing methods.

Growing medium: This can take the form of anything that plant roots are able to grow in. This generic term can be used to refer to soil or compost, as well as to inert mineral materials from which plants derive no direct benefit other than physical support.

But it is not just the plants that gain benefit from the soil. It is, in fact, a two-way relationship, as the formation of the soil and its continued health relies on all the things that live in it. Understanding this is important for the cultivation and success of raised beds, as well as any garden border or planted container you may have.

In nature, the growing cycle of plants starts with them taking water and nutrients from the soil and ends with them returning their dead remains where they can decompose and release nutrients. What is often overlooked is that plants have the ability to use the energy from sunlight to make their own food in the form of sugars, to fuel growth. And this means that when they die down at the end of their growing cycle, there is a net gain to the soil in the form of essential organic matter.

Not only that, but as the roots of plants grow into the soil, they open up its structure to aid both aeration and drainage. Meanwhile, the roots also secrete carbon into the soil and help to nourish its other forms of life.

Making the best use of natural soil, and optimizing its potential, is one of the greatest assets to the gardener and grower of plants in the long term. And successful raised-bed growing relies on filling them with a growing medium that will be ideal for the plants and good for the environment, as we'll discover (see page 194).

Acidity and alkalinity in soil

The composition of soil, how it has formed, and its origin will ultimately determine not only the nutrients that it contains, but also its chemistry. One of the most fundamental aspects of this is the concentration of hydrogen ions, measured for convenience on the pH scale.

Acidic soils tend to develop over granite rock, areas of heavy rainfall, and under waterlogged vegetation. As a result, the chemistry of the resulting

Benefits of organic matter

- Organic matter helps to hold the structure of the topsoil open to let water pass through, and also to provide aeration.
- It retains moisture in the topsoil – especially in hot, dry conditions.
- It intercepts rainfall and watering and thereby acts as a sponge to release water slowly into the soil beneath.
- It helps to catch and retain soil nutrients, preventing them from being washed from the soil.
- A fibrous layer of organic matter insulates the soil from the cold in winter and from excess heat in summer.
- When applied as a mulch to the surface it imitates what occurs in nature when dead leaves and other organic material fall to the ground.
- It feeds worms and other soil organisms to maintain soil health and fertility.
- Surface application smothers weed seeds to limit their germination.
- It slowly decomposes to release nutrients, which are recycled to plant roots.

Surface mulches of organic matter help to suppress weed growth and retain moisture in the soil.

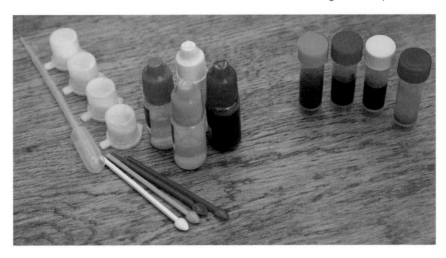

Take time to test not only the pH, but also the nitrogen, phosphorus, and potassium levels of the soil to reveal its nutrient status.

soil can lock up phosphate, while calcium, copper, magnesium, and potassium become easily washed away, particularly in soils with a pH of 5.5 or less.

Alkaline soils, which form over limestone or chalk rock, contain lots of calcium and magnesium, and this in turn results in a low concentration of hydrogen ions. Alkaline conditions can also form in very hot, dry climates. Such soils may lack available nutrients (elements) such as boron, copper, iron, manganese, phosphorous, and zinc, particularly at pH 7.5 or more.

Meanwhile, where soils have formed over clays and, in many cases, on alluvial deposits in river valleys, the pH is often around neutral – generally between pH 6.5 and 7. However, pH may be reduced in such places where rainfall is high, and increased where rainfall is very low.

In some instances, the pH of the soil may have been altered by farming or gardening activity. Applications of lime and some fertilizers can increase the pH and this is often carried out on naturally occurring acidic soils. In contrast, heavy applications of farmyard manure or sulphur may reduce the pH, causing it to become more acidic.

Testing your soil

It is hugely useful to test the existing soil in a garden, in order to determine which plants will naturally thrive in it. A good pH balance is something between 6 and 7, which will suit a wide range of plants and reduce the chances of nutrient deficiencies. Ericaceous plants, such as heathers and rhododendrons, will relish acidic conditions, while most vegetables benefit from being grown in soil with a pH of 6–7. By contrast, cherries, lavender, and lilac, for example, all grow better in a pH of 7 and above.

Testing your soil's pH, either professionally or with a kit, will identify its relative acidity or alkalinity, but bear in mind that soil can vary within a few metres, so test different parts of the plot where raised beds are to be built or where soil is to be taken for use.

It is also crucial to test soils for their major nutrient status. High levels of nitrogen will promote good leaf growth, but may also make them prone to weather damage, as well as pest and disease infestation; sufficient phosphorus is necessary for sustained root development and general plant health; while good levels of potassium are essential for flowering and fruiting, as well as balancing nitrogen to toughen up plant tissues to make them more weather resilient and less vulnerable to attack by pests and diseases.

Growing media for raised beds

Providing the best conditions for plants ultimately comes down to giving them the perfect growing medium to get their roots into. And mixing your own is the key to success.

There's no doubt that filling raised beds with topsoil will give better results than simply topping them up with a compost that is based solely on organic matter. While the latter might be suitable for growing plants in pots and smaller containers in the short term – just one to two years – it is far from ideal to make up large volumes in the longer term.

Any compost based purely on organic matter will quickly break down, causing the surface level to drop (see page 199). This doesn't happen in topsoil or a loam-based compost (composed of a fertile mix of sand, silt, and clay; see page 196), where the solid mineral matter maintains the structure despite the decomposition of any organic matter it contains. Nature can then be emulated by adding extra organic matter as a surface mulch every year to optimize growing conditions.

Pre-mixed topsoil blends and loam-based composts are readily available from garden centres and in bulk direct from suppliers. Bulk bags will work out as much more economical than small, individual bags.

Most will contain a baseline level of nutrients that will last for six to eight weeks. Subsequently, the decomposition of any organic matter they contain will contribute nutrients. Additional fertilizers can be applied where necessary in subsequent seasons (see Chapter 5, page 228).

Quality and health of the growing medium

Good-quality, healthy soil is the essence of all good growing and, as we've seen throughout this book, creating raised beds gives the opportunity to fill them with the growing medium that best suits whatever you choose to grow. The quality of that growing medium, however, can be a difficult thing to gauge, and it is important to understand what a bed needs to be filled with to ensure that it does the best job it can for the plant roots.

When getting hold of bulk materials for raised beds it is essential that they come from a reliable source. First and foremost, topsoil and organic matter need to be from sustainable and environmentally responsible origins, but they also have to be free from contamination. Certain chemical pesticide and weedkiller residues can remain in soil and organic matter, and if used to fill raised beds, these can affect crops and ornamentals. Such contaminants can slow, restrict, or kill plants, as well as being taken into both the natural and human food chain.

It's also crucial that the materials are free from pests and diseases, which could be transferred from the growing medium you are using to the plants that you are growing in the raised beds, seriously damaging their health.

Well-rotted organic matter is an essential constituent of any good growing medium (left); good-quality topsoil contains mineral matter, weathered from the underlying rock (right).

Topsoil mixtures

Based on good-quality, naturally occurring topsoil or loam, these may have additional, small quantities of organic matter (up to 10 per cent by volume) added to them to improve structure, help retain moisture, and maintain aeration. The best topsoil mixes are described as "sandy loam", which means they have an open, aerated, and free-draining structure. Check out the British Standard (or other national standards/guidelines) for topsoil. Beware of buying in topsoil from an unknown source.

Organic-matter composts

These include peat-based, reduced-peat, and peat-free versions. Some contain a low proportion of sharp sand or other drainage materials to add stability and to act as drainage material. They tend to be lightweight and will decompose over two to three years, losing their structure, aeration, and drainage properties in the process. Peat-free and reduced-peat composts can be variable in their quality and formulations, depending on the type of organic matter that is used to make them. They can be used to top up the organic-matter content on the surface of a raised bed but are not suitable for filling its whole volume.

Loam-based mixes

John Innes composts include loam (good-quality soil) as well as around 25 per cent organic matter (by volume); peat has been used for this in the past, but now, due to environmental concerns, peat alternatives should be used. Heavier than organic-matter compost, and soil-like, these compost mixes are good for permanent plantings in raised beds as they maintain their structure for a longer period than organic-matter composts.

Ingredients for growing media

In addition to good-quality garden soil and loam, there are a range of other constituents that can be combined with them to fill beds. All of these materials can be used to specifically tailor a growing medium to suit particular plants.

Inorganic matter

Garden soil
• Most domestic garden soil is good enough to provide the base for a raised-bed mix.
• It will usually contain mineral matter derived from the underlying local rock (see loam).
• Variable amounts of organic matter depending on the type and prior use of the soil.
• Bear in mind that the soil may have been imported from another source.

Loam
• Loam is considered to be an ideal soil with balanced proportions of mineral particle sizes.
• It is a mix of clay (particles of <0.002mm in diameter), silt (particles of 0.002–0.05mm), and sand particles (particles of 0.05–2.0mm).
• Ideal "sandy loam" is roughly 20 per cent clay, 40 per cent silt, and 40 per cent sand by volume.
• Available as different grades in bulk quantities.

Coarse or "sharp" sand
• Largest grade of pure sand is suitable for use in horticulture; no organic matter.
• Particle size ranges from 2.0–4.75mm.
• Mixed range of sizes helps to hold open the structure of the growing medium.
• Provides extra aeration and drainage in heavy topsoil.

Horticultural grit
• Small-grade quartz gravel specifically for horticultural use.
• Ranges in particle size from 1–6mm in longest diameter.
• Wider range of sizes than coarse sand to create density with drainage.
• Angular outline to ensure it maintains air and drainage spaces.

Crushed stone and gravel
• Medium grade. Varies in particle size from 5–50mm.
• Can be used as drainage material in the base of raised beds to prevent waterlogging in wet conditions.
• May be mixed into soil in small quantities to add extra weight and stability. Usually added to lower levels in raised-bed soils.
• Does different job to coarse sand or horticultural grit.

Expanded clay pebbles
• Made from aerated, fired clay to form porous pebbles for adding aeration and drainage to the growing medium.
• Lightweight material – different densities available too, from 250kg/cubic metre up to 510kg/cubic metre.
• Range of sizes, commonly 0.1–4mm, 4–10mm, and 10–25mm for raised-bed use.
• Can be used as a base layer for drainage or mixed into growing medium to bulk up topsoil.

Clean demolition rubble and large stones
• May be used to fill up to a quarter of the depth of very deep raised beds to take up volume cheaply.
• Avoid covering up any usable topsoil or subsoil when filling.
• A continuous layer of rubble in the base of a raised bed may improve soil drainage on heavy soils and areas of high rainfall.
• Large pieces of rubble or stone will not contribute to aeration or drainage when completely surrounded by topsoil.

Organic matter

Homemade garden compost
• Made from garden and kitchen waste, broken down in a compost heap or bin.
• Best made by combining two parts "brown" (woody) with one part "green" (leafy) waste (see page 224, for instructions on how to make it).
• Fibrous material, moisture- and nutrient-retentive.
• Contains good levels of major plant nutrients – nitrogen, phosphate, and potassium.

Green waste compost
• Produced by local authority schemes and commercial businesses.
• Most use domestic garden waste, sometimes adding other forms of woody and leafy material to aid decomposition.
• Fibrous material; may be coarser than homemade garden compost.
• Widely used as a soil conditioner to improve existing topsoil.

Composted agricultural waste

• Includes commercial composts made from the green waste produced as a by-product of field crops.
• Variable depending on the type of organic matter used in their production.
• May be more fibrous than homemade garden compost.
• Low-level nutrients released as material decomposes in the soil.

Coconut husk fibre

• By-product of the coconut farming industry in tropical regions of world. Also known as coir fibre.
• Husk fibres are washed, heat treated, chopped, and sieved to create fine compost material.
• Consistent material, moisture retentive, low in nutrients.
• Available as compressed blocks, which require rehydration before use.

Composted bark

• By-product of the forestry industry in various parts of the world.
• Chopped and stacked to compost. Various grades, of which fine is good to mix into soil.
• Holds some moisture. Oils and tannins in the bark mean that it is slow to decompose in soil, so good for aeration and drainage.
• Relatively low levels of nutrients.

Wood chip

• By-product of the timber industry, using chipped "brash" (forestry timber waste) and offcuts, not sawdust.
• Needs to be composted to avoid locking up nitrogen in the soil.

• Holds soil structure open. Once decomposition starts, it is quicker to rot down than bark.
• Relatively low levels of nutrients released back into the soil.

Spent mushroom compost

• Commercial by-product; the composted growing medium for mushrooms.
• Usually made from straw, and covered with an organic matter or soil "casing" layer.
• May contain lime in the "casing" layer, making it unsuitable for acid-loving plants.
• Moisture-retentive, but also free-draining.

Farmyard manure and livestock bedding

• By-product from animal farming. Sometimes referred to as FYM (farmyard manure). May contain variable amounts of bedding straw.
• May be relatively fresh, or partially or well rotted, depending on the source. Well rotted is preferable to avoid nutrient lock-up in the soil.
• Very high in nutrients, particularly nitrogen, which will encourage lush, vulnerable growth.
• Use in small amounts for certain crops and ornamentals, which require rich growing conditions in raised beds.

Leaf mould

• Made using collected and stacked leaves from trees and shrubs. Uses leaves from deciduous species in autumn, or those that fall from evergreen species, usually early in the growing season.
• Leaves are usually chopped and moistened to hasten the decomposition process.
• Takes up to two years to break down into leaf mould.
• Fine-grade material. Moisture-retentive, with relatively low levels of nutrients.

Pine needles

• Decomposed coniferous leaves or "needles". May be shredded before composting.
• Slow to decompose, so helps to hold soil open to aid aeration and drainage.
• Only moisture-retentive when well composted.
• Low in nutrients. May temporarily lower the pH of the soil until decomposed.

Logs

• Forms the basis of *Hügelkultur* (see Chapter 1, page 43).
• Can be used as a fill layer in the base of deep raised beds to reduce the cost of topsoil.
• Slow to decompose and release small amounts of nutrients to deep-rooting plants and to the soil organisms.
• Can aid drainage in the early years, and moisture retention when decomposing.

Mixing and filling

When it comes to getting the growing medium right, it pays to take a leaf out of nature's book and imitate the soil layers that develop with the cycles of the seasons.

The layers that build up in natural, undisturbed soils may have taken thousands of years to develop, but gardeners can usefully recreate these to fill raised beds. There is little point in filling a bed completely with an organic-based compost, as this will simply continue its decomposition process and lose its structure over the course of a few years (see opposite). Instead, the best approach is to put various topsoil and compost ingredients (see page 195) to good use by layering or grading them up through the raised bed.

What you decide to use will depend on the depth of the bed you are creating and the types of plants that you are intending to grow. Where possible, it is best to use good-quality topsoil to fill the majority of the volume of raised beds. Relatively shallow beds, those up to a maximum of 30–40cm (12–16in) high, can simply be topped up with a garden soil or bought-in loam mixed three parts by volume with one part organic matter in some form (see pages 196–197).

Where beds are taller than 30cm (12in) it is a good idea to dig out any existing topsoil from the area and then use this to mix into the new fill material. For beds more than 40cm (16in) tall where drainage is an issue, a greater depth of soil (including the subsoil) can be excavated and the hole filled with a layer of free-draining crushed builders' rubble or stone.

A layered approach

When filling beds it is important to do it in layers, around 15cm (6in) at a time, consolidating it with your heels to exclude large air pockets and to ensure that the growing medium maintains its capillary action and retains moisture. Put any excavated subsoil into the bed first, on top of the drainage layer (if used). Existing topsoil can then be combined with new topsoil or loam for adding in layers up to half the depth of the bed.

For the top half of the bed, it is a good idea to mix three parts (by volume) topsoil or bought-in loam with at least one part organic matter, as aforementioned. This will ensure that the structure of the growing medium stays sufficiently open to allow drainage and aeration, but also retains

Basic topsoil mix

Quantities are measured in parts by volume. Use a barrow, bucket, or sack for a rough measurement. It is not necessary to be too precise or to measure by weight.

3 parts good-quality topsoil

1 part coarse sand or horticultural grit

1 part fine organic matter

Additional organic matter can be added as a mulch after filling (see opposite).

Instructions

1
Combine three parts topsoil with one part coarse sand or grit and one part organic matter.

2
Mix together thoroughly.

3
Fill the bed in layers, firming in with the heels of your boots.

4
Add extra organic matter to the top as a mulch every year.

moisture for the plant roots. Alternatively use a commercial loam-based compost (e.g. John Innes) to fill the top half of the bed.

Additional drainage material should be mixed into the topsoil fill if needed for alpines, drought-tolerant species, and other plants that require a drier root run.

Such a layered approach to filling will mimic natural soil, with more mineral matter at the base to allow for drainage. Meanwhile, towards the top, increasing the amount of organic matter will retain moisture and help to hold on to nutrients. In addition, as it decomposes, it will release its own chemical elements into the soil for plants to use. It is then simply a matter of adding more organic matter each year in the form of a mulch to maintain the health of the topsoil.

Decomposition and settlement

Anyone who has filled a container with compost to grow plants knows the surface level drops with time, and the same happens in raised beds. This is due to settlement, caused by the weight of the medium compressing the air pockets lower down, and the breakdown of organic matter. In a raised bed, where plant and animal remains are tidied away, this nutritious decomposed material is not naturally replenished, so avoid filling beds with an organic-matter compost. Instead, mix it into the upper layers of mineral-rich topsoil or loam compost, which won't break down and will continue to provide aeration. Here, the organic matter will be used up but can be replaced yearly with a layer of mulch.

Weight considerations on buildings

The installation of raised beds on roofs and balconies needs careful consideration to avoid overloading and causing structural failure.

When considering a rooftop or balcony bed, it is easy to underestimate the combined burden of the growing medium and the plants themselves, as well as the additional weight of water that is held after rainfall or irrigation.

In some cases, flat roofs may have been specifically designed for load bearing and as usable basic domestic space, in which case they will usually have been constructed from reinforced concrete and fully tied into the building. It is the same with integrated concrete balconies on apartment blocks. This is no guarantee that either of these structures can take the extra weight of a raised bed, roof garden, or green roof, however.

The majority of domestic roofs are of lightweight timber or metal construction. In the case of flat

Lightweight materials for rooftops

Avoid using soil, loam, sand, and other heavy constituents for roof beds. Various mixes can be made to suit specific plants. A good general mix might be three parts (by volume) composted organic matter, three parts compost-grade chipped bark, and four parts pumice or perlite.

• Composted organic matter – various forms can be used to help retain moisture and nutrition in the mixture.

• Compost-grade chipped bark – this helps drainage, but also retains a limited amount of moisture.
• Expanded clay pebbles (Hydroleca) – made of aerated kiln-fired clay. They hold moisture and aid drainage.
• Pumice – a naturally occurring, crushed volcanic material, which is porous. It provides aeration as well as some moisture retention.
• Perlite – heat-expanded pumice granules, which help aeration and hold limited moisture.
• Vermiculite – heat-expanded, naturally occurring mineral. Readily holds moisture but does not contribute to drainage.

Organic matter

Expanded clay pebbles (Hydroleca)

Perlite

Vermiculite

Raised beds transform this roof into a green space, but it is crucial to check first that the structure can take the additional weight.

roofs, the roof supports are boarded and then covered with some form of waterproof membrane. Some balconies are also built from timber or metal. Meanwhile, pitched roofs may be stronger to carry the weight of tiles or slates.

In all cases, these structures are strong enough to provide occasional access for maintenance and possibly to allow personal use with lightweight furnishings, but not soil, water, and plants.

It is crucial that advice is taken from a structural engineer before adding plantable structures, and this includes pots and planters! Beefing up the roof or balcony supports may prove costly, but it's vital to the continued integrity of buildings.

Where sufficient load-bearing strength exists, the pitch or angle of a roof will affect the type of installation that it can accommodate. The steeper the pitch, the more likely the growing medium is to migrate or move down the slope due to rainwater impact and erosion.

Virtually flat roofs, with a very shallow pitch or an angle less than 10 degrees to the horizontal, are most suitable for deep beds planted with ornamentals or cropping vegetables. These usually have a level surface in which to plant and grow, so soil migration is not a problem.

On a steeper pitched roof, it may be an option to build a stepped system of shallow horizontal beds along its length. Meanwhile, turf and wildflower mixtures can be retained on a roof slope of up to 25 degrees, using a bed up to 15cm (6in) deep; however, this may require subdivision of the whole area into segments to help hold the growing medium in place.

For steeper pitches of up to 45 degrees, it is best to forego the raised bed in favour of a green-roof system, composed of succulent mats.

Finishing and styling raised beds

The surface of the soil in any raised bed can be finished in lots of different ways and for a range of different reasons. This can take the form of mulches (both organic and inorganic) and decorative finishes, as well as associated features and materials.

Cobbles and a water feature, made from a simple ribbed container, help create a stylish finish to this raised bed.

A mulch of well-rotted organic matter, a minimum of 5cm (2in) thick, is the most functional way to finish a raised bed. It can be used on its own or applied before another mulch or decorative layer is added. Beneficially, it will help to conserve moisture in the soil, prevent soil being splashed up onto the foliage and flowers, suppress the germination of weed seeds, and cover the spores of certain fungal diseases. We'll look at this in more detail in Chapter 5 (see page 231). Bear in mind, too, that the darker the colour of the mulching or finishing material, the more it will absorb sunlight energy, thus heating up the soil to promote early growth and to combat the effects of frost.

Homemade garden compost, commercial green compost, leaf mould, and spent mushroom compost can all be used for topping off raised beds in this way, around both ornamentals and edible crops. These will also provide nutrients to the plants as they continue to decompose on the surface.

Less decomposed forms of organic matter include chipped bark, pine needles and cones, cocoa shell, chopped straw, bracken, seaweed, and sheep's wool. They all provide cover on top of the soil to discourage weed growth and conserve moisture but will rot down slowly. Some of these have decorative merit, too, in particular chipped bark and cocoa shell, which provide a standardized, neutral surface finish. Not so good to look at are two other organic materials – newspaper and cardboard – though their abilities to aid weed suppression and water retention are both very useful.

Inorganic mulches

Where decorative effect is important, stone and mineral mulches can be used. They have the benefit of suppressing weeds, while allowing water to soak through and retaining it in the ground. The underside of larger stones also helps to keep the soil cool, particularly if they are pale in colour and therefore reflect the sunlight.

Cobbles and pebbles of different sizes can be laid in patterns or clusters to create stylish finishes among exotic plantings. Gravel, crushed stone, and crushed seashell can also be used with the added benefit that they may discourage slugs and snails from crossing the sharp surface to access vulnerable plants such as lettuce and other edibles, or hostas and soft-leaved perennials.

When it comes to using recycled materials, there are some useful inorganic mulches that may suit the design and style of a raised bed. Crushed and tumbled glass creates a bright, sparkling surface covering, which catches the sun and reflects it up under the leaves of plants and back to the viewer. The rounding of any sharp edges is essential in making this a viable option, but the tumbling process adds to the cost, making large-scale use prohibitive. Decorative patterns and swirls of the material used on cheaper gravel can add detailing, however, without busting the budget.

Surface covering can also take the form of geotextile materials or landscape fabrics. These are closely woven and thus provide a permeable barrier, which lets water drain through to the soil, but suppresses the growth of weeds through from underneath. Laid on the surface of the soil, planting holes can be cut into the material. Decorative stone mulch can then be put down to disguise the material, but avoid using organic mulch on the surface, as this will decompose and provide a foothold for the germination of weed seeds.

Depending on the design, theme, and planting of the raised bed, it is also possible to incorporate large rocks and even small water ponds or bog gardens. This is particularly effective for a specialist bed of alpines but can also look good with tropical foliage plants. Old tree stumps and branches make good materials for dressing the display, too.

Objects, containers, and water features can add sophistication, while recycled materials such as sinks, chimney pots, and decorative tiles can give a shabby-chic look to the finished bed.

This scheme has been finished with slate chippings and a seating hollow themed with colourful cushions for a stylish place to recline and relax.

Care and maintenance

Types of plants and how they grow

With so many different types of plant to grow, it can be difficult to understand what to expect from them and the best ways to sow or plant them in a raised bed – or indeed elsewhere in the garden.

Lots of plants that are grown seasonally in raised beds are considered as annual plants or crops. These include many types of vegetable, such as lettuce, radish, and rocket, and summer flowers like love-in-a-mist, Shirley poppies, and cornflowers. Once they have been harvested or flowered, the plants will die and need to be grown again from seed or bought as young plants.

Biennials also die once they've flowered or have been cropped, but their life cycle extends over more than one growing season. Germination and growth take place in the latter half of one year, with flowering to be completed in the next. Sweet Williams, foxgloves, and wallflowers are ornamental examples. In the meantime, many crops are grown as biennials – sowing them in one growing season to overwinter and then harvesting them early in the next. These include Brussels sprouts, winter leeks, and parsnips, all of which would produce flowers if left in the ground and go on to set seed, before returning into growth each year.

As for perennials, there are an enormous number of ornamentals that fall into this category, including varieties that bloom in every season of the year.

Annual edible crops such as lettuce may be sown multiple times in the growing season.

Explaining terms

The following terms are used to refer to the lifecycle of particular plants. They are often combined with an indication of the plant's hardiness to distinguish each plant further – thus a "tender perennial", as distinct from a "hardy perennial".

Annual: Any plant that grows from seed, flowers, sets seed, and dies within a single growing season. May be sown multiple times in the growing season for a succession of plants. Also used to refer to plants that are only grown for a single season but may be perennial, such as some tender perennials, which are grown in summer as annuals.

Biennial: A plant whose lifecycle spans a single winter or cold season, growing from seed in the summer and autumn of one year, and then flowering, setting seed, and dying in the spring of the

Herbaceous perennials, such as gaura, euphorbia, and salvia, will return each year.

Some brassicas, such as sprouts, cauliflower, and cabbage, can survive frosty weather for winter harvests.

following year. Alternatively, it can refer to plants that grow in the run-up to a hot, dry season and then flower, set seed, and die after.

Perennial: Able to return year after year. Can be further categorized as "short-lived" when the plant only lives for three to five years. The term "perennial" can refer to herbaceous plants or woody plants (see right).

Herbaceous: A plant that dies back to a basal clump of leaves or disappears below ground seasonally. This may be due to

a period of winter cold, or summer heat and dry conditions. The plant is able to grow, flower, and set seed within the growing season. Although usually used to refer to spring- and summer-flowering border plants, spring bulbs are also a type of herbaceous perennial.

Woody: Refers to trees and shrubs that make tough woody branches and trunks that are able to survive seasonal winter cold. They may drop their leaves (deciduous) or keep them (evergreen) throughout the winter period.

Summer-cropping salads, vegetables, and annual flowers are easy to grow from seed. Many can be sown direct into beds.

Although perennial, climbing beans are frost tender, so they won't survive the winter outdoors in cold climates.

They are divided into two groups: herbaceous perennials and woody perennials. In both instances, these range from hardy to tender, which will influence their use in raised beds according to the local climate conditions, the tender types needing to be kept frost free if they are to survive from year to year. Tender herbaceous plants include dahlias, tuberous begonias, and hedychiums (ginger lilies), while hardy herbaceous perennials range from aquilegias to hostas, and from peonies to rudbeckias and cannas, to name but a very few.

Meanwhile, perennial vegetables vary between the hardy globe artichoke (a clump-forming plant from which the giant flowers are harvested), half-hardy potatoes (whose tubers can be saved in a frost-free place to replant each season), and tender runner beans (which can regrow each year only if the roots are not killed by frost). In the vast majority of cases, perennial vegetables will be herbaceous, rather than woody.

When it comes to woody perennials – ornamental and fruiting trees, together with flowering shrubs and fruit bushes – these also fall into the frost-hardy and tender types. It is possible to grow any of these in all but the smallest of raised beds, but in the majority of cases they will require careful pruning to limit their size at the same time as optimizing their performance (see page 234).

Plant hardiness

There are a number of different ways of categorizing plant hardiness, some of which are overseen by recognized bodies in particular countries, with maps to show the regional temperatures to expect. Examples of this are the Royal Horticultural Society's hardiness charts in the UK or the hardiness zones developed by the United States Department of Agriculture (USDA). These can be very useful for specific plants, but they can also be complicated. A basic way of classifying the more common garden and indoor plants is as follows:

• Tropical: Needs temperatures of at least 10°C (50°F) to survive but requires a minimum of 16°C (61°F) to thrive.
• Tender: Can't survive frost and requires temperatures in excess of 5°C (41°F) to survive in winter, preferably above 10°C (50°F).
• Half hardy: Plant is able to survive very short periods in temperatures as low as -3°C (27°F) but ideally needs temperatures to remain above freezing.
• Hardy: Can survive long periods of sub-zero temperatures in winters down to -10°C (14°F).
• Very hardy: Plant is able to survive temperatures below -10°C (14°F) for prolonged periods.

Sourcing new plants for raised beds

Growing your own plants from seed, from cuttings, and by division is an economical way to fill a raised bed, plus you'll have the satisfaction that goes with it.

When it comes to sourcing the plants for raised beds, garden centres offer so much choice of instant-impact plants, which can be tempting, though it can also prove expensive to buy in this way. They may sell smaller plants and seeds, too, as a cheaper means of stocking borders, and the best centres will stock some more unusual varieties alongside the standard fare.

The best way to obtain less common plants is to track down nursery growers and seed stockists. Many of the things they offer aren't necessarily difficult to grow, so it's important not to be put off. They are a great way to try something a bit different, either by visiting in person or buying by mail order.

And there's no doubt that raising plants from seed, cuttings, and division is one of the most rewarding things about raised-bed growing, and about gardening in general.

Growing from seed

The biggest benefit of growing from seed is that you can produce large numbers of plants easily and cheaply. Hardy annuals, herbs, and summer vegetables are the easiest for a novice and are a great place to start. Look on the back of seed packs to identify their plant type.

Some easy-to-grow seeds – such as hardy vegetables and annual flowers and many other types of vegetables – can be sown directly into the raised bed where they are to grow. Daytime temperatures need to be at least 12°C (54°F) and at night no lower than 5°C (41°F) for good germination and seedling growth, which coincides with spring.

These kinds of seeds can also be sown under cover – indoors or in a greenhouse – from late winter onwards, and this gives you larger plants more quickly, which you can then plant outdoors. And tender plants will need to be raised indoors, too. Germination temperatures will vary for the seeds of different plants.

When sowing indoors, use pots, seed trays, or recycled plastic food trays, filled with three parts (by volume) peat-free compost to one part horticultural grit or sharp sand mix.

Top tips for sowing

- Follow the instructions on the seed packet carefully, or research the particular type of seed being sown.
- Not all seeds need covering with compost or soil. Sowing depth is important.
- Seed should always be sown sparingly to allow air to circulate and room for the seedlings to develop.
- Don't sow all the seeds in a packet at once. This will mean there are some in reserve in case germination fails.
- Sow vegetables and annuals for cut flowers in small batches at two-week intervals so that they develop in succession. This will avoid a glut all at once and spread the harvest over a longer period.
- Seeds need moisture, air, warmth, and light to germinate into healthy seedlings.

How to sow direct in raised beds

01
Fork through the soil surface to open it up. Use the tines of the fork to rake the soil level and then lightly firm the surface by tamping it down with the back of the fork or the back of your hand.

02
Use a trowel or the end of a short piece of cane to make a seed drill at the depth suggested on the packet. Make individual holes for large seeds, such as beans, peas, or sweetcorn.

03
Water each hole, or along the drill, to ensure that there is sufficient moisture to encourage quick germination.

04
Take a pinch of small seeds between thumb and forefinger and distribute evenly and thinly along the drill. For large seeds, sow one or two in each hole.

05
Draw the soil over the seeds and lightly firm in place. For large seeds, water again as they need lots of moisture to germinate.

New plants from division

Many herbaceous perennials, including bulbs, can be lifted at the end of the growing season, or in early spring, and split into divisions to make new plants for growing in raised beds. While the biggest benefit of doing this is that it creates free plants, it also means that favourites can be propagated from a known source. In addition, the original plants benefit from this treatment as it reinvigorates them. Not every herbaceous perennial can be divided easily, however. Those with a solid, corky crown, or single fleshy tap root, such as peonies, platycodon, or cimicifuga, are best left alone.

Most suitable are the clump-forming types, such as phlox, rudbeckia, and Michaelmas daisies, which bulk up in three to four years to make lots of growing points with fibrous roots attached.

Simply lift the parent plant and carefully knock or wash the majority of the soil from its roots. This may be enough for the clump to split into small divisions or individual bulbs, but some clumps will need coaxing apart. Use a pair of large border forks inserted back to back into the centre of the clump to lever it in two. For more solid roots, slice through the clump with a border spade, serrated knife, or even an old saw. Each division will need to have roots and a growing point of buds or leaves.

To replant the divisions, use a trowel or spade to make a hole that is deep and wide enough to accommodate the roots. With the plant in place, fill in with soil around the roots and firm well to leave the growing point just at the soil-surface level. Water well to settle the soil and encourage fresh root establishment.

Growing plants from cuttings

The stems of many plants can be used to make cuttings from which new plants can be grown to plant in raised beds. Although this requires some skill and experience, as well as pots and compost, it is a relatively cheap way of obtaining more plants. Existing plants in the garden or other raised beds could provide cutting material, but friends and neighbours may also be generous, too, providing a way to obtain new plants.

To take stem cuttings, always choose healthy material that is free from pests and diseases, and take the cutting from shoots that are of average size and vigour: weak stems are unlikely to have the energy to grow, while the most vigorous shoots will usually wilt or rot before they get a chance to root. It is also beneficial to remove the very soft tip of a shoot, where the leaves are not fully developed, as this will tend to take valuable energy from the cutting and thereby reduce the chances of it rooting successfully.

There are four basic types of stem cuttings that can be taken – softwood, greenwood, semi-ripe, and hardwood, according to the time of year and state of growth (see below). These different types will be suitable for specific plants, but bear in mind that some plants are very difficult or even impossible to root.

When should you divide?

As a rule, it is best to divide spring- and early-summer-flowering herbaceous perennials immediately after flowering or in the autumn. This allows them time to re-root before the following season. Plants that flower from mid-summer to autumn are best left to die down and overwinter, before lifting and splitting before growth starts in early spring.

10 plants to divide in autumn (or immediately after flowering)
- Astrantia
- Delphinium
- Dicentra
- Erigeron
- Hellebore
- Iris
- Leucanthemum
- Lupin
- Spring bulbs
- Pulmonaria

10 plants to divide in spring
- Aster
- Echinacea
- Geranium
- Helenium
- Helianthus
- Kniphofia
- Miscanthus
- Monarda
- Rudbeckia
- Solidago

Many woody plants can be raised from summer cuttings rooted in pots or in a raised bed filled with an equal-parts mix of sieved peat-free compost and sharp sand.

Softwood cuttings are the quickest to root and can be taken from the youngest shoots of many herbaceous and woody perennials early in the growing season, or from new growth at any time of year. Greenwood cuttings are usually taken in late spring or early summer, from the same types of shoots, once they have become less pliable but are still green.

On woody plants, further development of the new shoots will cause the base of them to become firmer or semi-ripe, and may be denoted by a colour change from green to russet or tan. By the end of the growing season, woody stems of the current year's growth will be fully ripened, with a thin coating of bark on the outside, which is referred to as "hardwood". This last type of material is usually taken in the dormant season when many woody plants have lost their leaves.

Most cuttings are made by cutting just above a leaf node at the top and just below a node at the base using a sharp garden or craft knife: softwood, greenwood, and semi-ripe cuttings are usually 5–10cm (2–4in) long, which will consist of between two and five nodes. Carefully cut the leaves from the bottom two-thirds of the cuttings. Insert them around the edge of a pot filled with a mix of equal parts (by volume) sieved peat-free compost and sharp sand. Make a pilot hole in the compost with the end of a pencil or cane, and push in the end of the cutting so that the bottom of the remaining leaves sit just above the compost surface. Lightly firm the compost around the base of the cutting and water well. Cover the pot with an inflated polythene bag or place in a propagator, and position on a windowsill indoors or in a greenhouse to root.

Perhaps easiest of all, however, are hardwood cuttings of particularly woody plants, which are taken at the end of the growing season: 20–25cm (8–10in) long, pencil-thick woody stems. Make a slot in the soil using a spade and insert the cuttings so as to leave the top 5cm (2in) above the surface. Firm the soil around the cuttings, water thoroughly, and leave them to root until the following summer.

Plants to grow from cuttings

Gain confidence with growing by taking softwood or greenwood cuttings. It is a great way to bulk up your supply of extra plants from existing ones or new purchases. Try propagating the following:

- Dahlias
- Fuchsias
- Argyranthemums
- Pelargoniums
- Penstemons
- Shrubby salvias

213

How to plant raised beds

Getting plants in the ground is the crowning glory of any raised-bed scheme. After the planning, designing, building, and filling has been done, the process of making holes in the earth is something to relish and not rush. Whether it's planting large specimens that will quickly bring results or small, young plants that need nurturing, each one comes with promise.

As with any aspect of gardening, it pays to be prepared and to have everything you need to do a proper job and give the plants the best chance of survival. A trowel, spade, and border fork are essentials, but it is possible to improvise for smaller plants with a large, old metal spoon.

Healthy soil, which has plenty of organic matter, will provide enough nutrients at planting time, but make sure the soil is moist. In temperate climates, planting is best carried out in the spring for annual and perennial flowers, summer-flowering bulbs, vegetables, and fruit. Autumn is best for spring-flowering bulbs and perennials, trees, shrubs, and fruit bushes. In warmer climates, planting can be carried out at any time, but preferably during periods of rainfall and not during the hottest months of the year.

It is also worth planting in the cool of the evening, so that the plants have a chance to settle in before the heat of the following day. Alternatively, plant early in the morning, but avoid the six-hour period either side of midday.

Autumn and spring are the best times of year to plant herbaceous perennials, shrubs, trees, and fruit bushes.

Well-developed roots are important for rapid establishment to support top growth after planting.

Mycorrhizal fungi

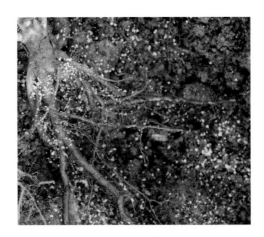

In most cases, plant roots can grow under the soil surface even in cold winter weather.

All plants have strong connections with the moisture and nutrients in the earth through their roots, but many have direct symbiotic links to other soil organisms, including fungi and bacteria. Such symbiosis involves a plant living in a connected way with another organism for mutual benefit.

One of the most important of these are the threads, or mycorrhizae, of certain types of fungi. They are particularly prevalent among the roots of woody perennials (trees and bushes), but some herbaceous perennials and even annual plants have been shown to have associations with mycorrhizae, too. The mycorrhizae connect to the roots and act in a similar way by taking up water and nutrients, which then make their way into the plant. In return, the plants supply the fungi with sugars that they are unable to make themselves.

In natural, undisturbed soils, these beneficial mycorrhizal fungi exist in abundance, but in neglected garden soils and new topsoil, they are lacking. Commercially available, they can be added in small amounts to the soil at planting time to aid establishment and stronger growth. They can also help make plants more drought resistant.

Prepare the ground by lightly forking it through to remove weeds and relieve any surface compaction. Don't be tempted to dig (see page 25), and only fork down to half the depth of the fork's tines. This will help to aerate the very top surface, while leaving the moist soil undisturbed lower down. In dry weather water the area to be planted thoroughly the day before.

At planting time, pot-bound plants (where roots are densely packed inside the pot and lots are growing out of the drainage holes at the base) will benefit from their roots being carefully teased apart to encourage them to grow out in the surrounding soil once they are in the ground.

An intimate connection is required between the plant roots and the soil, so make sure that all plants are well firmed and watered thoroughly. In all cases, planting should involve making sure that the roots of plants are well covered with soil to keep them moist, while stems and leaves should be above the surface where they can get air and light to grow. Aim to plant at the same depth at which the plant was growing in its pot or previously in the ground.

Sprinkling mycorrhizal fungi around the roots at planting time can be beneficial to many plants.

Planting in raised beds ... plug plants

Vegetables, bedding plants, herbaceous perennials

Available in a range of sizes from seedlings to young plants; it's worth potting up the smallest to grow on before planting out. Larger plugs can go straight into the ground.

Stand the plugs in water for five minutes to fully wet the compost they are growing in, before carefully removing them from trays or packaging.

01

Make a small hole in the soil using the tip of a trowel or an old serving spoon. Set the roots of the plant in the hole and carefully fill around them with soil, then lightly firm and water.

02

Pot up small seedlings in gritty compost to grow on to a larger size. They can be planted out as small pot plants (see page 218) in three to four weeks. Water in well once planted.

Delicate lettuce plugs can be directly planted out in raised beds or grown on in pots first.

Planting in raised beds ... pack-grown plants

Vegetables, bedding plants, herbaceous perennials, soft fruit

Multiple plants can be bought or homegrown in pack trays. Widely available in different sizes, all the plants will have a well-developed root ball to grow away quickly after planting.

01
Soak the root balls of the packs for 10 minutes to reduce damage to the roots when removing them. When ready to plant, push the base of each pack unit to remove the plant.

02
Use a trowel to make a hole large enough to accommodate the root ball of the plant so that its top ends up level with the surrounding soil.

03
Return soil around the roots of the plant and firm it carefully in place on all sides. Water the plants thoroughly once they are all planted.

Pack-grown pansies are readily available to buy, easy to plant up, and instantly colourful.

217

Planting in raised beds ... small pot plants

Vegetables, bedding plants, herbaceous perennials, succulents, soft fruit, young shrubs, seedling trees

Individual plants in their own small pot of soil or compost. These tend to be larger and more developed than pack-grown plants; they may be in flower if ornamental and will establish quickly.

01
First, soak the root ball in the pot for 10 minutes. Meanwhile, fork in some coarse horticultural grit to the soil for succulents and other plants that require free-draining conditions.

02
Dig a hole using a trowel or small border spade, making it large enough to comfortably accommodate the root ball so that the top sits level with the surrounding soil surface. Knock the plant from the pot. If roots are tightly circling the compost, carefully tease them apart to promote wider rooting.

03
Spread out any teased-apart roots and return soil around the root ball, firming in layers. Make sure the top of the root ball is just covered to keep it moist.

When planting up succulents, such as Aeonium, add plenty of horticultural grit to the soil.

Planting in raised beds ... bulbs, corms, and tubers

Spring flowering, summer flowering, tuberous vegetables

Usually sold generically as "bulbs", these can take the form of true bulbs, corms, and tubers. They all require deep planting to prevent them drying out and to provide stability.

01
Unpackage the bulbs, corms, or tubers and discard any with signs of damage or rot. If dry, soak in water for 2–3 hours to start the rehydration process.

02
Aim to plant the bulbs in a hole three times as deep as the height of the bulb. In this case, the bulbs will need to go in a hole made to the full depth of the trowel shown; smaller bulbs can go in shallower holes, while larger bulbs will need to be planted deeper.

03
Make a hole to the appropriate depth with a trowel to plant each individual bulb, or use a border spade to make a larger hole for multiple bulbs.

04
Place each bulb, pointed end uppermost, in the hole created, before covering it with the excavated soil and lightly firming in place.

Daffodil bulbs offer a reliable and delightful display of flowers in early spring.

Planting in raised beds ... herbaceous plants

Herbaceous perennials, perennial vegetables, soft fruit

Available as "liners" (small pots, see page 218) and in various pot sizes – the larger the pot, the bigger the clump, which can often be split to make more than one plant.

01

Prepare the soil for planting by forking in well-rotted organic matter to the depth of the tines of a border fork. Stand plants in water for 20 minutes to thoroughly wet the compost.

02

Using a trowel or border spade, dig a hole to a suitable size that will allow a 5cm (2in) gap around the root ball of the plant and is deep enough to leave the top of the root ball 2cm (¾in) below the surrounding soil level. Carefully knock the plant from its pot.

03

Tease apart any congested roots, put the plant in the hole, and backfill with soil, firming in layers. Create a shallow dish in the soil surface around the base of the plant to funnel water to the roots.

01

02

03

Herbaceous perennials, such as pulmonaria, heuchera, and salvia, are reliable and easy to grow.

Planting in raised beds ... shrubs, trees, and fruit bushes

Ornamental shrubs and trees, fruit trees and bushes

Always plant trees when small, not more than 1.4 metres (4½ft) high, and shrubs when young. These will establish more quickly than larger specimens and will result in a bigger plant in only a couple of seasons.

01

Soak the plant for 30 minutes. Dig a hole bigger than the root ball, allowing a 10cm (4in) gap at its edges. Aim to make a flat-bottomed, square hole, about 3–4cm (1¼–1½in) deeper than the plant's root ball.

02

Lightly fork the base of the planting hole, add a couple of handfuls of well-rotted compost, then mix it into the soil.

03

Set the root ball in place, then backfill around the roots with soil, firming in layers. Create a shallow dish at the soil surface around the base of the plant to direct water to the roots. Water thoroughly to settle the soil and promote root establishment.

The hardy shrub Osmanthus provides elegant evergreen foliage for a raised-bed scheme.

01

02

03

Maintaining soil condition and health

The most important aspect of successful gardening is about not only creating a good growing medium in the first place, but also keeping it in good condition.

Maintaining a good, open structure to your soil relies on an ongoing supply of organic matter being fed in at the top of the bed; without it, as we discovered in Chapter 4 (see page 199), the level of the topsoil will sink as the organic matter decomposes and is used up.

In nature, the yearly cycles of vegetative growth and decay mean that there is a regular topping-up of this essential ingredient. In a raised bed, however, in common with the wider garden, the supply of organic matter is controlled by the actions of the gardener and is best provided in the form of a surface mulch every year.

Avoiding deep cultivation

This forms the basis of the "no-dig" system of growing (see page 25), which promotes only minimal disturbance of the soil in order to maintain its natural structure as developed by the soil composition, the micro-organisms it contains, and plant roots. Deep cultivation in the form of digging and over-forking opens up this structure, making it more freely drained and aerated, exposing any organic matter to more rapid decomposition.

Yearly applications of organic matter on the surface ensure that soil is well maintained and forming the connections that are essential for good plant growth and health. Minimizing cultivation also extends to seed sowing and planting: light surface forking should be all that is necessary in well-conditioned, mulched soil to enable sowing drills and planting holes to be made. The latter only need to be the size of the pot the plant is growing in.

After filling beds, it pays to avoid deep digging so as to maintain a good structure for drainage and aeration.

Add organic matter to the surface of the soil in raised beds at least once a year to help maintain a good, open structure and to provide nutrients for the plants.

Home composting is easy, cost effective, and good for the environment.

The type of organic matter used to top up beds will influence the chemistry, the soil organisms, the availability of nutrients, and the overall structure of the topsoil itself. Bear in mind the differences in fibre content as well as the proportion of different nutrients: some materials will suit the needs of certain plants more than others. When it comes to ornamental plants, for example, species that have their origins in deciduous woodland will ideally benefit from leaf mould that is produced from deciduous trees and contains the partially decomposed remains of autumn leaves and woody twigs.

Meanwhile, mulching with composted pine needles can create a more open, aerated, and free-drained topsoil, and lower its pH, making it suitable for ericaceous (acidity-loving) plants. By contrast, adding spent mushroom compost as a mulch may gradually increase the alkalinity due to the lime used in the growing process. (For more on the best and most easily available composts for topping up the available organic matter in no-dig raised beds, see Chapter 4, page 196.)

Making your own compost

Any form of growing, whether in the open garden, in raised beds, or indoors, will benefit from home composting. Not only does it provide a useful source of organic matter for soil improvement, but it also recycles nutrients within the growing environment. This results in a huge cost saving on both bagged soil conditioners and plant fertilizers. And, in fact, it makes smart reuse of any additional fertilizers that you might have added previously and which are contained in the plant remains that have be composted.

It makes sense for the environment, too, as it reduces the carbon emissions and particulate pollution involved in transporting the green waste away and its mechanized processes. Add to that the fuel-use impact of bringing compost or sources of organic matter back to the plot for soil improvement, and cutting out all these processes by home composting results in big environmental savings. There are hidden wins, too, for the soil environment in maintaining its local biological diversity in the form of recycling soil organisms back into it.

Prunings, weeds, and faded leaves and flowers provide a valuable source of green material for the compost heap.

prunings, dried twigs, bracken, straw, dried foliage, eggshells, human and pet hair, ink-free cardboard and shredded paper, as well as pure woollen and cotton clothing. Meanwhile, green materials include such things as grass clippings, soft green prunings, vegetable and fruit peelings, and the seed-free tops of weeds.

Seasonal supply is one of the major limitations to successful composting so it is crucial to stockpile the raw materials as they become available so that they can be added to the compost heap in the correct proportions, by volume.

Home composting also allows you to monitor what is going into the compost and therefore what comes out in the soil, in terms of chemicals, plastic wastes, weed seeds, and roots. Any of these might make their way into commercial green waste composts, unless the production processes are carefully monitored.

Simple recipe for success

The science of composting is based on the chemistry that occurs in both the carbon and nitrogen cycles. Both of these chemicals need to be present in some form to enable decomposition.

Put simply, it is about getting the balance of brown and green materials right. The browns contain carbon and the greens contain nitrogen. Then, in moist, warm, and well-aerated conditions, with the help of soil organisms, the recipe for creating good, homemade compost will be complete. Yet again, this is the science of nature. Autumn leaves are naturally a balance between green and brown, so can rot down readily.

For the home composter the raw ingredients should be in the proportion of two parts brown to one part green. The brown includes woody

Compost like a pro

It is possible to make decent compost in as little as 10 weeks with ideal ingredients and weather conditions, as well as the time to spend on caring for the heap. Expect it to take an average of six to nine months under variable conditions.

• Avoid putting on large quantities of one type of material – for example, woody prunings in the winter or grass clippings in the summer.
• Add mixed batches of brown and green material from stockpiles.
• Apply 5–10cm (2–4in) layers at 7–10 day intervals if a mix of materials is available.
• Mix the top 30cm (12in) every 10–14 days using a border fork.
• Turn the whole compost heap every 6–8 weeks, if possible, to aerate and speed up the process.
• Cover the heap in winter to keep out cold rain and to maintain heat inside.
• Water the contents in hot, dry weather and cover with a layer of damp, corrugated cardboard to retain moisture.
• Use at least two compost bins, where space allows, to allow one to rot down thoroughly when full.

Plants and watering

Providing plants with sufficient water is the most crucial aspect of raised-bed growing, but it can also be one of the hardest things for a gardener to get right.

Watering can be tricky because not only do the water requirements of particular plants vary, but the prevailing conditions affect the amount of water they lose from their leaves and thus the amount they need to take up to replace it.

What is often overlooked is that plant roots need air as well as moisture to stay healthy. Roots need to take up oxygen from that air to store energy in the form of sugars in their cells. This energy allows for the effective functioning of the cells and enables the plants to take up nutrients. So it is important not to overwater.

And, as ever, looking to nature will demonstrate how cultivated plants can be best watered. The soil in which plants are rooted is subject to periods of rain, which soaks into the ground and then drains away. As it does so, this water is absorbed by the organic matter and, as any excess drains down, it pulls air into the soil surface behind it. This alternate wetting and aeration of the soil is how both water and oxygen get to plant roots. And mimicking this natural cycle is the most successful approach to use for watering.

Getting water to raised beds

Delivering additional water to plants needs to be done as efficiently as possible. You can carry water from butts and tanks in watering cans to where it is needed, but this represents a huge physical effort for some. Instead, hosepipes can be fed by solar-powered pumps or by gravity from tanks higher on the plot.

Use hosepipes carefully to optimize water usage and its benefit to the plants, particularly if you choose to use mains water from a tap. Direct the water down onto the soil at the base of plants to allow it to soak down where it can be of most use, rather than giving a quick sprinkle over the foliage. This is particularly important in raised beds as it is the soil that stores and supplies the plants with their essential moisture.

There is a boggling array of watering devices, automatic watering systems, and sundries available. Micro-drip or seep-hose systems deliver water at the base of plants where it can readily drain down into the soil for the roots to use. Timers enable them to be turned on during the evening, night, or morning so the water has time to soak in rather than evaporate. Meanwhile, sprayers and sprinkler systems are generally much more wasteful. The small droplets of water they produce can readily

Direct water to the base of each plant so it can soak down to the roots where it is needed.

A soaker or leaky hose threaded between young plants can dribble water efficiently into the soil.

What needs to be watered?

• Seedlings and young plants can dry out rapidly and shrivel, especially in hot weather and before they have a chance to root more deeply into the soil of a raised bed.

• Newly planted specimens, particularly large ones, will need additional water in dry weather during their first couple of seasons.

• Plants that have shallow roots – vegetable crops as well as annual, biennial, and some herbaceous perennial flowers – are prone to drying out in hot, dry weather at any time during the active growing season.

• Indoor plants rely on the grower to supply all the moisture that is available to them, but the growing medium should not be kept permanently saturated.

• Established trees, shrubs, and fruit bushes that are able to root out into the soil underneath a raised bed can tap into the underground reserves of water. Where raised beds are made on a solid base, however, these plants will need additional watering in order to stay alive.

evaporate into the air, although timed application overnight is more efficient.

Water is a scarce resource in many parts of the world, and using mains tap water to irrigate plants contributes to diminishing river levels and underground aquifers, with huge environmental consequences. In addition, the treatment and pumped supply of "potable" or drinking water to homes uses resources that impact on the climate and the environment. Using rainwater is not only better for the planet, but also for the health of plants, as additives to mains water can be damaging to roots and the micro-organisms in the soil.

How plants are "plumbed in" to the soil

It is a necessary evil that in order to take up water by their roots, plants also need to lose it through their leaves and stems via small pores in their surface. Water moves into the roots through tiny root hairs, which form an intimate connection with the particles of soil to extract water from them. The water then moves up through the plant in the form of sugary sap and ultimately provides the molecules of water needed for photosynthesis. This is the process by which the water is combined with carbon dioxide and uses sunlight to create oxygen and energy in the form of sugar.

This flow of water is called the transpiration stream, which also helps to hold plant stems and their leaves upright. Thus, anything that interrupts the flow will cause the plant to wilt, whether it be too little or too much water at the roots.

What's in the water?

One of the greatest advantages of saving rainwater to use on plants is that it is free from treatment additives and is only very slightly acidic, which means that it can be used on any plants. By comparison, mains water supplies are tapped from a wide range of different sources, including reservoirs, rivers, and underground aquifers. This means that its pH can vary widely depending on the rocks it has come into contact with. In addition, lime may have been added in the treatment works, together with other chemicals, to make it safe for us to drink. This means that on naturally ericaceous soils, or in raised beds filled with lime-free soil, the pH can be altered if the soil is watered with an alkaline mains supply.

Rainwater is, therefore, especially handy for watering raised beds filled with ericaceous plants, such as rhododendrons and camellias.

A tip from dry-climate growers

Getting water to soak into the soil before it runs off the surface or evaporates is a particular problem in dry climates or during very hot weather. The creation of a shallow depression, or "dish", in the surface of the soil around the base of individual plants can help to direct water to where it is most needed and is particularly useful during the initial stages of establishment.

On a larger scale, mounding soil up around the inside edges of a raised bed to make a water-retaining sump will cause a large volume of water to pool around it, allowing it to soak into the ground to benefit all its plants. This takes its inspiration from flood irrigation schemes used in agriculture and horticulture around the globe.

If mains water has to be resorted to, aim to use watering cans, rather than hosepipes and sprinklers.

Wise use of a natural resource

• Install water tanks and butts on all rainwater downpipes to catch supplies at times of high rainfall.
• Reused or "grey" water that has been used for preparing vegetables in the kitchen, washing, and showering is suitable for watering plants outdoors. Avoid reusing water that has excess soap residues or detergents in it or potentially toxic cleaning chemicals.
• Use drought-tolerant plants in raised beds and other plantings, rather than those that are particularly water-thirsty.

• Create shade in hot, sunny locations by planting small trees or large shrubs to protect raised beds from the heat of the day and thus reduce water loss.
• Aim to cover up the soil with the foliage of plants. This will deflect the sun's rays from the soil's surface and trap a layer of moist air under the leaves to reduce evaporation.
• Apply any additional water in the cool temperatures of the early morning or late evening so it can soak down into the soil to be used by the roots of plants.

Soak the soil at the base of plants so the water goes deep into the soil. This will encourage deep rooting, making the plants more self-sufficient in the longer term.

Plant nutrients

As a gardener or grower it can be tempting to anthropomorphize plants and treat them like ourselves or our pets, especially when it comes to providing nutrition. This is often referred to as "feeding" plants, but it's important to remember that we can also overdo it.

With the availability of so many commercial plant "foods", it's easy to get carried away with feeding our plants. Despite the name, however, it is crucial to remember that plants are able to make their own food in the form of carbohydrates, via photosynthesis using sunlight energy. What they do benefit from is additional nutrients, which are the raw materials used to make their roots, stems, leaves, flowers, and seeds, as well as the hormones that control growth.

In nature, these chemical nutrients are obtained from the soil and, as we've already seen, are recycled in the form of organic matter and minerals from weathered rocks (see page 191). In cultivation they can be used up and not readily replaced so that plants grow less well and can be prone to pests, diseases, and extremes of weather.

Rotating crop plants can go some way to making full use of the nutrients that accumulate in the soil over more than just a single season. Peas and beans, for example, are able to "fix" nitrogen into the soil thanks to the bacteria-containing nodules in their roots, so following them with a leafy, nitrogen-hungry crop such as lettuce or chard makes sense.

Raised beds are often cultivated more intensively, however, and the plants grown in them may benefit from applications of additional nutrients, in the form of plant "foods" or fertilizers. This can't be seen as an alternative or replacement for organic matter. The latter is crucial for acting as a sponge to hold onto the nutrients, as well as maintaining the soil moisture into which the nutrients can dissolve, for absorption by the plant roots.

Using fertilizers

Powdered or granular fertilizers are best sprinkled onto the surface of the soil and gently hoed in, to allow rain or watering to dissolve them and take them down to the roots. Meanwhile, liquid fertilizers are watered onto the roots or leaves and therefore act more quickly but for a shorter period.

Slow-release or controlled-release fertilizers are also available. Here, the effects of the fertilizer are delivered over a longer period – up to three months in some cases.

For best results, it pays to use the right fertilizer for the right plant, at the right time: nitrogen at the start of the growing season, potash in the middle, and phosphate pretty much anytime the plants are actively in growth. When growth occurs over a longer period or, in warmer climates, all year round, applications can be made over a longer season.

Above all, don't overdo it. Follow the instructions on the fertilizer packaging for how much and how often to apply. Not only can nutrients be wasted, but plants are actually better off with no additional nutrients than too many, as too much fertilizer can lead to a build-up of chemical salts, which may draw moisture out of the plant. Keep soil well maintained with organic matter and it should not be necessary to add much in the way of extra nutrients.

Follow the instructions on packaging carefully when applying commercial fertilizers, as well as wearing any protective clothing that is indicated.

Liquid fertilizers are mostly diluted in water prior to application. In most cases, they can also be applied in spray form to the plant's foliage.

Pelleted manures are a good, general-purpose form of nutrients to maintain the health of plants. Only apply them during periods of active plant growth.

Slow-release fertilizer granules are coated so that they will only provide nutrients during appropriate growing weather.

Plant nutrients and what they do

Nitrogen (N)
• Promotes cell division to make new roots, leaves, shoots, and other structures.
• Essential for making the green chlorophyll that plants need to make food from sunlight.
• A lack of nitrogen may result in weak growth and yellowing of foliage.
• Too much nitrogen can deter flowering.
• Very soluble in water and easily washed from the soil or compost in wet weather.

Phosphorus (P)
• Aids root and tuber formation, as well as enabling roots to take up other nutrients.
• Helps to transport other nutrients around the plant.
• Used in the leaves and stems to help release the energy from carbohydrates made by the plant and maintains health.
• Deficiency can result in small leaves, a purplish coloration to the foliage, and fruit that is slow to mature.
• Deficiency is rare as phosphorus doesn't wash out of soil.

Potassium (K)
• Essential for the formation of flowers, seeds, and fruit.
• Balances the effects of nitrogen by toughening cell walls – both in plant tissues and in the formation of wood.
• This toughening makes the plant less prone to extremes of heat and cold, pests, and diseases.
• Deficiency is most common on light, sandy soils and signs include brown scorching and the curling of leaf tips.

Calcium (Ca)
Makes micronutrients (see below) available that would otherwise be chemically "locked up" (i.e. made unavailable to the plant by being chemically bonded to minerals or compounds in the soil). Usually applied in the form of lime to neutralize acid soils. Used in early spring, if needed, but not at the same time as organic matter, with which it can adversely react.

Micronutrients
• Vital nutrients, including iron (Fe) and magnesium (Mg), are needed regularly in small quantities for plant health.
• Deficiency of certain nutrients can produce growth disorders in particular plants, including the discoloration of leaves.

Trace elements
• Wide range of minerals (selenium, molybdenum, and even gold) are needed in minute quantities for optimal growth, human health benefits, and flavour in fruit and veg.
• Mulches of homemade garden compost usually provide all that's needed. Some brands of organic fertilizer also contain trace elements.

Healthy leaves, like those on this ruby chard, rely on a good source of nitrogen, as well as other nutrients.

Simple ways to deal with weeds in raised beds

Unwanted plants are usually referred to as weeds and will compete with desirable species for space, light, moisture, and nutrients in raised beds.

Tackling weeds in raised beds can be done in a number of different ways:

• Hand-weeding involves pulling weed seedlings and young plants from the soil. A garden trowel or hand fork can be used to loosen the ground immediately around the base of the unwanted plant in order to remove the roots. This is used to control both annual and young perennial weeds. It is important to keep soil disturbance to a minimum to lessen the risk of turning up new weed seeds to the surface.

• Digging out roots of established perennial weeds is a more time-consuming job. Some have deep tap roots that need to be dug out to their entire length, while many others have wide-spreading roots or rhizomes, which need to be traced and teased out of the soil. Breaking these roots or leaving sections in the ground will allow them to regrow.

• Hoeing involves slicing through the surface of the soil to cut off the top growth of seedling and young weeds. Different types of hoe are used for this, but all rely on having a narrow, sharp-edged blade, which chops the top growth of the weed from its roots. Hoeing is best done in dry weather so that the top growth can be left on the soil surface to wilt and wither. The roots of annual weeds will not regrow and, in most cases, neither will the seedlings of perennials.

• Mulching offers a great way of limiting weed growth in raised beds using compost, bark, or stones to reduce the germination of weed seeds. The mulch can be put down on top of a closely woven weed-suppressant material, which prevents seedlings and the regrowth of perennial weeds from pushing up through it.

• Areas of otherwise bare soil can be cleared of weed seedlings and young plants by applying intense heat from a flame gun to burn and kill the foliage. Meanwhile, chemical weedkillers are less appropriate for use in raised beds, as they can readily get onto the foliage of adjacent cultivated plants and kill them, too. Spot treatment of the foliage of deep-rooted perennial weeds with a systemic weedkiller may be possible.

Pulling up weeds by hand while they are young means they can't flower and set seed.

Pests and diseases

Good gardening and hygiene are the essentials of pest and disease prevention. This involves clearing up the fallen leaves of infected plants, removing damaged stems, planting at the correct spacing, and using mixed plantings to reduce the chances of problems occurring.

When growing vegetables in raised beds, crop rotation can be a huge boon in helping to control plant problems. This involves grouping similar crops together, and then, each growing season, moving them around the sections to lessen the chances of reinfection by pests and diseases.

In addition, there are naturally resistant species and varieties of plants, as well as those that have been specifically bred to be able to shrug off the worst effects of pests and disease – or pathogens. Choosing to grow such plants can drastically reduce the problems the gardener might face over the growing season.

Using physical deterrents such as netting, mesh, or even solid barriers may be all that's needed to keep some plants healthy. The simplest of these is a fruit cage to guard against bird damage, while individual fruits can be covered with muslin or old stockings as a deterrent to wasps. Other innovative barrier methods include planting crops under environmental mesh to stop flea beetle and other sap-sucking insects getting at them, as well as collars of carpet, underlay, or cardboard around the neck of brassica seedlings to ward off root fly.

Meanwhile, raised beds of 80cm (31in) high will deter carrot root fly, which is unable to fly that high. In some cases, it is worth disguising the smell of

Caterpillars can quickly decimate crops if left to their own devices (top). Environmental mesh or netting is a good physical barrier against flying pests (bottom).

crops (or even ornamentals) with other strongly scented plants. For example, mint alongside carrots, cabbages, and onions will deter a specific pest of each, namely carrot fly, flea beetle, and onion fly.

Chemical control

Where plant pest or disease infestations escalate very quickly, there are chemicals available to buy for use in their control. It is crucial to bear in mind that such chemicals may not only kill pests and diseases, but beneficial organisms as well. Organic products are also available to buy, and while perceived as acceptable to use, they can also damage or kill other beneficial organisms.

Where gardeners do choose to use chemicals, applications should be made responsibly to minimize the amount used, optimize their efficacy, and lessen the chance of resistance. Applying a limited amount of chemical to a small pest or disease infestation in a very targeted area may be much less damaging to beneficial organisms and the surrounding environment than a prolonged and widespread application when the problem has got completely out of control. Safe and responsible storage of garden chemicals is also crucial. They should be kept in a locked cabinet, out of reach of children and animals.

An open, sunny site will help to reduce incidence of fungal diseases, such as powdery mildew on peas.

Creating a natural balance

• There is natural balance between all living things. As pest numbers increase, populations further up the food chain will increase to keep them in check.
• Such biological control takes many forms, whether it be some of the more obvious examples, such as birds eating insects, larvae, and their eggs, or amphibians and hedgehogs eating slugs.
• There are lots of smaller species that prey on garden pests. Hoverflies, ladybirds and their larvae, and spiders all do their bit to keep pest numbers down.
• A certain level of a pest species is necessary to support the populations that feed on them. It takes patience and faith in

nature for this to be a success, as well as an understanding that it won't STOP pests entirely, but control their numbers.
• Other forms of biological control are available to buy, including parasitic wasps to deal with whitefly and aphids, while predatory mites are used on red spider mite, fungus gnats, and some types of thrips. Other introductions include microscopic nematodes for use against slugs, vine weevils, leatherjackets, and chafer grubs.
• The key to success with biological control is to avoid chemical sprays, as these will often kill the beneficial wildlife or the imported biological control itself.

Pruning and cutting back

Knowing how to cut back, or prune, is vital for keeping your plants in good shape and preventing raised beds from becoming overgrown – something that is crucial for producing the best display from the minimum space.

Cutting woody plants back hard in the dormant season or just before buds burst has the effect of encouraging strong vegetative or leafy stem growth. At the same time, it removes all the previous growth so that the plant doesn't get too large.

This drastic-looking technique is used every year for plants that are able to produce flowers at the ends of new growth. In temperate areas this includes summer-flowering shrubs, such as butterfly bush (buddleia) and shrubby mallow (lavatera).

It is also used on woody plants that are grown for their colourful new-growth stems – in particular the bark of cornus and willows. These shoots will have the strongest colour once the leaves fall from the plants in autumn.

In addition, such hard pruning before growth starts can be used on woody plants that are grown for large, dramatic foliage. Hard pruning concentrates all the plant's growth into fewer buds, and some plants will produce not only vigorous stems, but huge leaves as well.

Pruning out the new, soft growing tips of tree and bush fruits directs essential moisture into the swelling fruit and lets in sunlight to ripen it.

Why prune plants?

There are a number of different reasons why gardeners prune plants, especially woody shrubs, trees, and fruit bushes. They can cut plants in order to:

• control their size and shape
• encourage more flowers and fruit
• extend their life
• control pests and diseases
• deal with damaged parts
• remove dead and dying material
• promote decorative effects – stem colour, leaf size, particular form
• remove "reverted", untypical growth or suckers
• create dense growth for topiary
• tidy up growth after flowering or at the end of a particular plant's growing season

Hard pruning should not be used for woody plants that bloom on growth made in the previous season, however, such as philadelphus, forsythia, or weigela. These are best pruned immediately after they have finished flowering – which is usually early in the growing cycle, or the spring in temperate regions (in the case of fruit bushes, pruning should wait until after the fruit has been picked). For these plants, the oldest flowered or fruited stems – usually three years old – are cut down to their base using a pruning saw, with the strongest younger stems left in place to flower in subsequent years. Any weak, spindly stems are also removed so that the plant's energy is channelled into worthwhile growth.

Cutting back is also done on a wide variety of herbaceous perennial plants at the end of their growing cycle. This can be done after flowering to tidy the plants up, but in some cases – as with alliums, rudbeckias, and achilleas – the foliage and seedheads left after flowering can be decorative in their own right.

A number of herbaceous perennials that flower early in the growing season can also be cut back after they have bloomed in order to produce another flush of growth consisting of fresh foliage and, sometimes, more flowers – aquilegias, geraniums, and lupins, for example.

Cutting back herbaceous plants like this perennial geranium after flowering can allow them to produce a second flush of blooms.

Off with their heads

Deadheading keeps plants looking their best, whether they are annuals, alpines, herbaceous perennials, or shrubs.

It is particularly useful for plants that have been bred to produce large-petalled flowers and double blooms. These often retain their petals as they fade, turning yellow and then brown. In wet conditions, the remains of flowers can create a slimy mess and encourage the development of fungal infections, which can

result in stem die-back. Aim to check your plants at least a couple of times a week and use secateurs or snips to remove faded blooms as and when you see them. But remember not to cut back any plants that have a second season of interest, in the form of hips or berries, as deadheading will prevent these from forming later in the year.

Snipping out faded blooms keeps roses tidy and puts energy into new flower buds.

Index

Page numbers in *italics* refer to illustrations

Picture credits

The publisher would like to thank the following for their kind permission to reproduce their photographs:

(Key: a-above; b-below/bottom; c-centre; f-far; l-left; r-right; t-top)

Alamy Stock Photo: Ingrid Balabanova 30, Botany vision 25, Anna Carpendale 83cb, Chris Clark 214, De Agostini / P. Jaccod / Universal Images Group North America LLC 87br, Johan De Meester / Arterra Picture Library 17, Hannes Eichinger 35, Environmental Stock Images by Streeter Photography 188tl, Flowerphotos 89bc, Clare Gainey 215br, Tim Gainey 224, gardenpics 18, Granger - Historical Picture Archive 14tl, Heinz Hauser / botanikfoto 176, 227, Historica Graphica Collection / Heritage Images 14tr, Saxon Holt 188tr, Wayne Hutchinson 46, Mark Hodson Photography 15, Jeremy Pembrey 48; **Richard Bloom:** 2b, 8-9, 52-53tc, 110, 201; **Sarah Cuttle:** 78, 122, 141, 186, 187tl, 216b; **Dorling Kindersley:** Peter Anderson 85cl, 85br, 105clb, Peter Anderson / Trehane Nursery 67br, Alan Buckingham 57c, 57cr, 233, Mark Winwood / Ball Colegrave 72bc, Brian North / Thompson and Morgan 85c, Mark Winwood 72cr, Mark Winwood / Hadlow College 85cr, Mark Winwood / John Hall Plants, Hindhead 67tl, Mark Winwood / RHS Chelsea Flower Show 2014 65tc, 65cl, Mark Winwood / RHS Wisley 65cr, 67tc, 70, 72tc, 72tr, 72br, 79br, 83crb, 85tl, 85bl, 85bc, 87bc, 89tc, 89tr, 89cl, 89c, 93clb, 93crb; **Dreamstime.com:** Darko Plohl 206, Alessandro Termignone 89cr; **GAP Photos:** 33, 73crb, 77tl, 125, 126, 132bl, 134, 137tl, 145r, Matt Anker / Designer: Sara Edwards 184, Richard Bloom 115t, Richard Bloom - Garden: Kings Cross Roof Terrace - Designer: Emily Erlam Studio 116b, Richard Bloom - Katharina Nikl Landscapes 145cla, Mark Bolton 132tr, Elke Borkowski 177t, Elke Borkowski - Design: David Domoney 129, Christa Brand 64bl, Chris Burrows 175crb, Leigh Clapp - Designer: Nic Howard 20, Leigh Clapp - Show Garden GW5. Design Credit: PaulMartinDesigns.com 53cra, Simon Colmer 106, Design - Cube 1994 112crb, Paul Debois 63tr, 63br, Heather Edwards 120cr, Heather Edwards - Design: Nick Williams-Ellis 56bl, Heather Edwards - Design: Robert Myers 183t, FhF Greenmedia 113tl, Tim Gainey 60, 63tl, 76bl, 160bl, Annaick Guitteny 172, Marcus Harpur - Garden: Kiftsgate Court Gardens 21, Modeste Herwig - Designer: Erik van Gelder 143, Martin Hughes-Jones 120tr, 158, Andrea Jones 174cr, Andrea Jones - Design: Tony Smith 203, Robert Mabic 16, 41, 96bl, 104, Caroline Mardon - Garden: Walpole Gardens - Designer: Karen Rogers www.krgardendesign.com 100bl, Fiona McLeod 136cb, Clive Nichols - Designer: Ana Sanchez-Martin of Germinate Design 97tl, Brian North 128bl, Brian North - designer Chris Parsons 96tr, Nova Photo Graphik 67bl, Anna Omiotek-Tott 99tr, 103tl, Anna Omiotek-Tott - Design: Rhiannon Williams 167tr, Anna Omiotek-Tott - Design: Tom Massey 88, Anna Omiotek-Tott - Designer: Andy Bending 133, Hanneke Reijbroek 102crb, Hanneke Reijbroek - Chaumont sur Loire 2014 113cra, 124, Howard Rice 54, S &

O 118, J S Sira - Designer: Ian Hammond. Sponsors: Squires Garden Centre 49, Gary Smith 115clb, Nicola Stocken 19, 56tr, 96-97bc, 100br, 102cla, 131, 175cra, Nicola Stocken - Designer Laura Arison and Amanda Waring 166, Nicola Stocken - NHS Tribute Garden. Designer: Naomi Ferrett-Cohen 111t, Stephen Studd - Designed by Jane Grenan & David Lewis 97cb, Ian Thwaites 83tr, Visions 67bc, Evgeniya Vlasova 67cr, Juliette Wade 137br, Juliette Wade / Roger Gladwell Landscapes 123, Brent Wilson 98bl, 98br, Mark Winwood 117tr; **Getty Images:** mikroman6 12; **Getty Images / iStock:** brytta / E+ 81, Pauws99 32, powerofforever / E+ 13, SolStock / E+ 39, taikrixel 27, timltv 45, Vaivirga 127, yoh4nn 34; **Jason Ingram:** 55tr, 113cl, Designer: Joshua Fenton 167tl; **Matt Soper, Hampshire carnivorous plants Ltd:** 86; **Marianne Majerus Garden Images:** Marianne Majerus / Chelsea Physic Garden, London 180, Marianne Majerus / Design: Acres Wild 128br, Marianne Majerus / Design: Bunny Guinness 179tr, Marianne Majerus / Design: Emma Griffin 111bl, Marianne Majerus / Design: Gabrielle Evans / African Vision: Malawi Garden, RHS Hampton Court Flower Show 2015 183, Marianne Majerus / Design: James Aldridge 82, Marianne Majerus / Design: James Smith 53crb, Marianne Majerus / Design: Peter Berg 181, Marianne Majerus / Design: Stuart Craine 178, Marianne Majerus / Design: Tom Stuart-Smith 182, Marianne Majerus / Design: Miles Raybould 2tr; **Shutterstock.com:** NayaDadara 42, NokHoOkNoi 215tl.

Author's acknowledgements
There are so many people who have contributed directly and indirectly to this book. Most obvious are Sarah Cuttle for her photography, and Barbara and Alan Wells, Erika Savory and Ade Sellars for making their gardens available for photoshoots. Meanwhile, I'd like to thank Chris Young for his encouragement, and all those who have shared the creative journey. Finally, and posthumously, credit should go to Major and Mrs Youens, and more especially to Dorothy, Jim, Vera, and Norman, who nurtured my green fingers.

Publisher's acknowledgements
Dorling Kindersley would like to thank our Raised Bed Heroes – **Thomas Berolzheimer**, **Mark Diacono**, **Doris Kampas**, **Anja Klein**, **Anya Lautenbach**, **Emma Lovewell**, and **Patrick Vernuccio** – for sharing their inspired planting plans, gardening wisdom, and general love for growing in raised beds. DK would also like to thank Chris Young for his kind permission to photograph in his garden; Myriam Meguarbi and Emily Hedges for picture research; Neil Hepworth for additional photography; Nick Jordan for repro work; Vanessa Bird for indexing and Kathy Steer for proofreading.

DK LONDON
Editorial Manager Ruth O'Rourke
Senior Designer Glenda Fisher
Senior Editor Alastair Laing
Designer Jordan Lambley
Production Editor David Almond
Senior Production Controller Stephanie McConnell
Jacket Design Jordan Lambley
Art Director Maxine Pedliham
Publishing Director Katie Cowan

Consultant Gardening Publisher Chris Young
Editorial Holly Kyte
Design Geoff Borin, Christine Keilty
Photography Sarah Cuttle
Illustration Paohan Chen, Daniel Crisp

First published in Great Britain in 2024 by
Dorling Kindersley Limited
DK, One Embassy Gardens, 8 Viaduct Gardens,
London, SW11 7BW

The authorised representative in the EEA is
Dorling Kindersley Verlag GmbH. Arnulfstr. 124,
80636 Munich, Germany

A CIP catalogue record for this book
is available from the British Library.
ISBN: 978-0-2416-4872-8

Printed and bound in China

www.dk.com

MIX
Paper | Supporting
responsible forestry
FSC™ C018179

This book was made with Forest Stewardship Council™ certified paper - one small step in DK's commitment to a sustainable future. **For more information go to www.dk.com/our-green-pledge**